Plácido Domingo

Consulting Editors

Rodolfo Cardona
professor of Spanish
and comparative literature,
Boston University

James Cockcroft
visiting professor of Latin American
and Caribbean studies,
State University of New York at Albany

Hispanics of Achievement

Plácido Domingo

Rebecca Stefoff

Chelsea House Publishers
Philadelphia

CHELSEA HOUSE PUBLISHERS

Editor-in-Chief: Remmel Nunn
Managing Editor: Karyn Gullen Browne
Copy Chief: Mark Rifkin
Picture Editor: Adrian G. Allen
Art Director: Maria Epes
Assistant Art Director: Howard Brotman
Manufacturing Director: Gerald Levine
Systems Manager: Lindsey Ottman
Production Manager: Joseph Romano
Production Coordinator: Marie Claire Cebrián

Hispanics of Achievement
Senior Editor: John W. Selfridge

Staff for PLÁCIDO DOMINGO
Copy Editor: Joseph Roman
Editorial Assistant: Danielle Janusz
Designer: Robert Yaffe
Picture Researcher: Joan Beard
Cover Illustration: Robert Caputo

7 9 8 6

Library of Congress Cataloging-in-Publication Data
Stefoff, Rebecca
    Plácido Domingo/Rebecca Stefoff.
      p. cm.—(Hispanics of achievement)
    Includes bibliographical references and index.
    Summary: Profiles the life and career of the Spanish opera singer
who is also known in the world of popular music.
    ISBN 0-7910-1563-7
          0-7910-1692-7 (pbk.)
    1. Domingo, Plácido, 1941– —Juvenile literature. 2. Singers—
Biography—Juvenile literature.
[1. Domingo, Plácido, 1941– . 2. Singers.] I. Title. II. Series.
ML3930.D6S8 1992   91-32358
782.1'092—dc20   CIP
    [B]   MN AC

Contents

Hispanics of Achievement

Oscar Arias Sánchez
Costa Rican president

Joan Baez
Mexican-American folksinger

Rubén Blades
Panamanian lawyer and entertainer

Jorge Luis Borges
Argentine writer

Juan Carlos
King of Spain

Pablo Casals
Spanish cellist and conductor

Miguel de Cervantes
Spanish writer

Cesar Chavez
Mexican-American labor leader

El Cid
Spanish military leader

Roberto Clemente
Puerto Rican baseball player

Salvador Dalí
Spanish painter

Plácido Domingo
Spanish singer

Gloria Estefan
Cuban-American singer

Gabriel García Márquez
Colombian writer

Pancho Gonzales
Mexican-American tennis player

Francisco José de Goya
Spanish painter

José Martí
Cuban revolutionary and poet

Rita Moreno
Puerto Rican singer and actress

Pablo Neruda
Chilean poet and diplomat

Antonia Novello
U.S. surgeon general

Octavio Paz
Mexican poet and critic

Javier Pérez de Cuéllar
Peruvian diplomat

Pablo Picasso
Spanish artist

Anthony Quinn
Mexican-American actor

Oscar de la Renta
Dominican fashion designer

Diego Rivera
Mexican painter

Linda Ronstadt
Mexican-American singer

Antonio López de Santa Anna
Mexican general and politician

George Santayana
Spanish philosopher and poet

Junípero Serra
Spanish missionary and explorer

Lee Trevino
Mexican-American golfer

Diego Velázquez
Spanish painter

Pancho Villa
Mexican revolutionary

CHELSEA HOUSE PUBLISHERS

INTRODUCTION

Hispanics of Achievement

Rodolfo Cardona

The Spanish language and many other elements of Spanish culture are present in the United States today and have been since the
country's earliest beginnings. Some of these elements have come
directly from the Iberian Peninsula; others have come indirectly, by
way of Mexico, the Caribbean basin, and the countries of Central
and South America.

Spanish culture has influenced America in many subtle ways,
and consequently many Americans remain relatively unaware of
the extent of its impact. The vast majority of them recognize the
influence of Spanish culture in America, but they often do not
realize the great importance and long history of that influence.
This is partly because Americans have tended to judge the Hispanic
influence in the United States in statistical terms rather than
to look closely at the ways in which individual Hispanics have
profoundly affected American culture. For this reason, it is fitting

that Americans obtain more than a passing acquaintance with the origins of these Spanish cultural elements and gain an understanding of how they have been woven into the fabric of American society.

It is well documented that Spanish seafarers were the first to explore and colonize many of the early territories of what is today called the United States of America. For this reason, students of geography discover Hispanic names all over the map of the United States. For instance, the Strait of Juan de Fuca was named after the Spanish explorer who first navigated the waters of the Pacific Northwest; the names of states such as Arizona (arid zone), Montana (mountain), Florida (thus named because it was reached on Easter Sunday, which in Spanish is called the feast of Pascua Florida), and California (named after a fictitious land in one of the first and probably the most popular among the Spanish novels of chivalry, *Amadis of Gaul*) are all derived from Spanish; and there are numerous mountains, rivers, canyons, towns, and cities with Spanish names throughout the United States.

Not only explorers but many other illustrious figures in Spanish history have helped define American culture. For example, the 13th-century king of Spain, Alfonso X, also known as the Learned, may be unknown to the majority of Americans, but his work on the codification of Spanish law has greatly influenced the evolution of American law, particularly in the jurisdictions of the Southwest. For this contribution a statue of him stands in the rotunda of the Capitol in Washington, D.C. Likewise, the name Diego Rivera may be unfamiliar to most Americans, but this Mexican painter influenced many American artists whose paintings, commissioned during the Great Depression and the New Deal era of the 1930s, adorn the walls of government buildings throughout the United States. In recent years the contributions of Puerto Ricans, Mexicans, Mexican Americans (Chicanos), and Cubans in American cities such as Boston, Chicago, Los Angeles, Miami, Minneapolis, New York, and San Antonio have been enormous.

The importance of the Spanish language in this vast cultural complex cannot be overstated. Spanish, after all, is second only to English as the most widely spoken of Western languages within the United States as well as in the entire world. The popularity of the Spanish language in America has a long history.

In addition to Spanish exploration of the New World, the great Spanish literary tradition served as a vehicle for bringing the language and culture to America. Interest in Spanish literature in America began when English immigrants brought with them translations of Spanish masterpieces of the Golden Age. As early as 1683, private libraries in Philadelphia and Boston contained copies of the first picaresque novel, *Lazarillo de Tormes*, translations of Francisco de Quevedo's *Los Sueños*, and copies of the immortal epic of reality and illusion *Don Quixote*, by the great Spanish writer Miguel de Cervantes. It would not be surprising if Cotton Mather, the arch-Puritan, read *Don Quixote* in its original Spanish, if only to enrich his vocabulary in preparation for his writing *La fe del cristiano en 24 artículos de la Institución de Cristo, enviada a los españoles para que abran sus ojos* (The Christian's Faith in 24 Articles of the Institution of Christ, Sent to the Spaniards to Open Their Eyes), published in Boston in 1699.

Over the years, Spanish authors and their works have had a vast influence on American literature—from Washington Irving, John Steinbeck, and Ernest Hemingway in the novel to Henry Wadsworth Longfellow and Archibald MacLeish in poetry. Such important American writers as James Fenimore Cooper, Edgar Allan Poe, Walt Whitman, Mark Twain, and Herman Melville all owe a sizable debt to the Spanish literary tradition. Some writers, such as Willa Cather and Maxwell Anderson, who explored Spanish themes they came into contact with in the American Southwest and Mexico, were influenced less directly but no less profoundly.

Important contributions to a knowledge of Spanish culture in the United States were also made by many lesser known individuals—teachers, publishers, historians, entrepreneurs, and others—with a love for Spanish culture. One of the most significant of these contributions was made by Abiel Smith, a Harvard College graduate of the class of 1764, when he bequeathed stock worth $20,000 to Harvard for the support of a professor of French and Spanish. By 1819 this endowment had produced enough income to appoint a professor, and the philologist and humanist George Ticknor became the first holder of the Abiel Smith Chair, which was the very first endowed Chair at Harvard University. Other illustrious holders of the Smith Chair would include the poets Henry Wadsworth Longfellow and James Russell Lowell.

A highly respected teacher and scholar, Ticknor was also a collector of Spanish books, and as such he made a very special contribution to America's knowledge of Spanish culture. He was instrumental in amassing for Harvard libraries one of the first and most impressive collections of Spanish books in the United States. He also had a valuable personal collection of Spanish books and manuscripts, which he bequeathed to the Boston Public Library.

With the creation of the Abiel Smith Chair, Spanish language and literature courses became part of the curriculum at Harvard, which also went on to become the first American university to offer graduate studies in Romance languages. Other colleges and universities throughout the United States gradually followed Harvard's example, and today Spanish language and culture may be studied at most American institutions of higher learning.

No discussion of the Spanish influence in the United States, however brief, would be complete without a mention of the Spanish influence on art. Important American artists such as John Singer Sargent, James A. M. Whistler, Thomas Eakins, and Mary Cassatt all explored Spanish subjects and experimented with Spanish techniques. Virtually every serious American artist living today has studied the work of the Spanish masters as well as the great 20th-century Spanish painters Salvador Dalí, Joan Miró, and Pablo Picasso.

The most pervasive Spanish influence in America, however, has probably been in music. Compositions such as Leonard Bernstein's *West Side Story*, the Latinization of William Shakespeare's *Romeo and Juliet* set in New York's Puerto Rican quarter, and Aaron Copland's *Salon Mexico* are two obvious examples. In general, one can hear the influence of Latin rhythms—from tango to mambo, from guaracha to salsa—in virtually every form of American music.

This series of biographies, which Chelsea House has published under the general title HISPANICS OF ACHIEVEMENT, constitutes further recognition of—and a renewed effort to bring forth to the consciousness of America's young people—the contributions that Hispanic people have made not only in the United States but throughout the civilized world. The men and women who are featured in this series have attained a high level of accomplishment in their respective fields of endeavor and have made a permanent mark on American society.

The title of this series must be understood in its broadest possible sense: The term *Hispanics* is intended to include Spaniards, Spanish Americans, and individuals from many countries whose language and culture have either direct or indirect Spanish origins. The names of many of the people included in this series will be immediately familiar; others will be less recognizable. All, however, have attained recognition within their own countries, and often their fame has transcended their borders.

The series HISPANICS OF ACHIEVEMENT thus addresses the attainments and struggles of Hispanic people in the United States and seeks to tell the stories of individuals whose personal and professional lives in some way reflect the larger Hispanic experience. These stories are exemplary of what human beings can accomplish, often against daunting odds and by extraordinary personal sacrifice, where there is conviction and determination. Fray Junípero Serra, the 18th-century Spanish Franciscan missionary, is one such individual. Although in very poor health, he devoted the last 15 years of his life to the foundation of missions throughout California—then a mostly unsettled expanse of land—in an effort to bring a better life to Native Americans through the cultivation of crafts and animal husbandry. An example from recent times, the Mexican-American labor leader Cesar Chavez has battled bitter opposition and made untold personal sacrifices in his effort to help poor agricultural workers who have been exploited for decades on farms throughout the Southwest.

The talent with which each one of these men and women may have been endowed required dedication and hard work to develop and become fully realized. Many of them have enjoyed rewards for their efforts during their own lifetime, whereas others have died poor and unrecognized. For some it took a long time to achieve their goals, for others success came at an early age, and for still others the struggle continues. All of them, however, stand out as people whose lives have made a difference, whose achievements we need to recognize today and should continue to honor in the future.

Plácido Domingo

Plácido Domingo, photographed during the 1970s. After making his operatic debut in 1961, Domingo embarked on a career that has included more than 2,000 live performances in 30 years and earned him a place among the greatest tenors of all time.

CHAPTER ONE

The Mouth of the Wolf

I*n bocca al lupo* is Italian for "into the mouth of the wolf." The phrase is traditionally used to wish opera singers good luck, in the same way that people often encourage actors before they go on-stage by telling them to "break a leg." On May 19, 1961, in the city of Monterrey in northern Mexico, stagehands and colleagues were saying "in bocca al lupo" to a tall, dark-haired 20-year-old singer who was standing backstage, silently praying to St. Cecilia, the patron saint of musicians, while he waited for the opera to begin.

The young man's name was Plácido Domingo. He was about to walk out in front of the audience—into the mouth of the wolf—to attempt his first performance in a leading operatic role. The evening was to hold several surprises for him.

The opera being performed that night was *La traviata*, com-posed in 1853 by Giuseppe Verdi. It is a dramatic love story that contains much beautiful music, and for more than a century it has been one of the great popular favorites at opera houses around the world. Verdi's opera was considered scandalous, however, when it was first performed in Venice, Italy. *Traviata* means "wayward woman" or "fallen woman" in Italian, and the leading female character is a lovely and elegant courtesan, or prostitute, named Violetta.

The story, set in Paris, is simple: In the first act, Violetta throws a lavish party at which she is introduced to a handsome young man named Alfredo Germont. In a stirring aria, or solo song, Alfredo tells Violetta that he has fallen in love with her. She tells him that she is not interested in serious love but only in gaiety and pleasure, and then, before she sends him away, she reveals to the audience in a long and passionate aria that she has only a few months to live.

In the second act, Violetta has fallen in love with Alfredo and has left Paris to live with him in a country house. One day when Alfredo is away, Violetta receives an unexpected visit from his father, who tells her that Alfredo's relationship with her is disgracing his entire family. He pleads with her to break with Alfredo, and Violetta tearfully agrees. She writes a note telling Alfredo that they must part forever, and then she returns to Paris. Alfredo, deeply wounded by Violetta's mysterious behavior, decides that she never loved him and that she must have missed the company of her former wealthy lovers; later, when he sees her with one of them in Paris, he insults her cruelly.

In the third and final act, Violetta is dying of tuberculosis. Alfredo's father has finally told his son the true reason that Violetta left him. Alfredo rushes to Violetta's bedside to beg her forgiveness. The two sing a passionate duet, and Violetta dies in Alfredo's arms.

The story of *La traviata* may be simple, but producing it—or any other opera—onstage is a complex matter indeed. Opera was born in Florence, Italy, around the year 1600 and was at first conceived of as a type of performance that would unite the arts of music, drama, dance, and painting. As opera evolved over the years, different aspects of the performance gained or lost prominence; solo singers, for example, became more important than choruses, and dance ceased to play a significant part in most operas. Even though the relative importance of the various elements has changed somewhat since the origin of opera, the successful performance of an opera still depends on the smooth interaction of a number of individual artists in different disciplines.

Every opera performance is a fusion of many elements—music, which is performed by an orchestra under the leadership of a conductor; singing, which is the responsibility of the soloists and the chorus; acting, in which the singers are coached by the stage director or production designer; the sets, or scenic backdrops, which must be designed, built, painted, and maneuvered; costumes, which for some operas must suggest distant countries or long-ago eras; lighting, which must be arranged to reflect the interaction among the performers and also to show the sets to best advantage; and props, objects such as furniture and weapons, which sometimes merely decorate the set and at other times contribute to the plot of the opera.

Most people would agree that the singing is the most important aspect of an opera, the standard by which the whole performance is judged. Yet opera at its best is a precisely timed effort by dozens, perhaps hundreds, of individuals, coordinated to the split second. And as Domingo discovered during his debut, a slipup in any detail can have far-reaching consequences.

In the second act of *La traviata,* after Violetta has spoken with Alfredo's father, Alfredo returns home and finds her missing. After puzzling over her whereabouts, he hears someone coming and sings, "There's someone in the garden. Who is it?"

At this point, a messenger is supposed to come onto the stage, singing, "A lady in a carriage, a little way from here, gave me this note for you."

On the night of his operatic debut, Domingo had performed well in the first act. The audience applauded his love song to Violetta, and his confidence grew as the performance progressed. During the second act, at the moment when he is supposed to hear the messenger arriving, he trustingly sang the lines "There's someone in the garden. Who is it?" But to his dismay, nobody appeared in the stage doorway. On that particular night, the man who was playing the part of the messenger simply failed to show up, and no one had noticed his absence until it was time for him to go onstage.

The lore of opera contains many tales of performances rendered hilarious or confusing by cues and props gone wrong. The tenor Leo Slezak—who was known to love wisecracks onstage— was appearing at New York's Metropolitan Opera in the role of Lohengrin, the Swan Knight, in Richard Wagner's opera *Lohengrin.*

The legendary Italian tenor Enrico Caruso, photographed in 1910 in costume for I pagliacci. *An exuberant performer with a keen sense of humor, Caruso was known to improvise imaginatively when things went awry during his opera performances.*

At one point he was supposed to glide into view on a giant swan—in actuality a mechanical boat that rolled along the stage on a concealed track. On this particular night Slezak missed the cue for his entrance and failed to get into the boat in time. The contraption sailed into view with no one in it. As the conductor and orchestra struggled to cover the knight's embarrassing absence with music, Slezak could be heard calling out, "What time does the next swan leave?"

Another misadventure at the Met involved soprano Renata Scotto, who was starring in Giacomo Puccini's opera *Tosca*. At the end of this opera, the character Floria Tosca, learning of her lover's execution, is supposed to hurl herself from a high tower. Directors stage this by having the soprano jump down onto a thick mattress that is hidden from the audience behind and below the scenery. On New Year's Eve, 1969, Scotto sang her passionate finale, ran up to the parapet—and simply stood there while the rest of the cast and the audience looked on in puzzlement. After the performance, Scotto explained her failure to jump: Someone had forgotten to put the mattress in its accustomed place.

Even Enrico Caruso, considered by many to have been the finest opera singer of all time, had his problems onstage. Once, in Puccini's *La fanciulla del west* (The Girl of the Golden West), he was supposed to shoot an enemy with a pistol that fired blanks. The prop gun would not fire; Caruso, thinking quickly, threw it aside in disgust, pointed his finger at his adversary, and shouted, "Bang!" The other singer obligingly clutched his chest and keeled over.

At the time of his debut as Alfredo, Plácido Domingo had appeared in only 11 opera performances, and in none of them had he played a leading role. Yet he had a family heritage of experience in zarzuela. Zarzuela, which originated in central Spain during the 18th century, combines elements of popular musical comedy and opera; its closest English-language equivalent would be the operettas of Gilbert and Sullivan.

During his childhood in Spain and Mexico, Domingo had watched his parents perform, and as a teenager he had taken roles in some of their zarzuela productions. Undoubtedly, he had seen his share of stage mishaps and knew that a botched scene could sometimes be salvaged with quick thinking and clever improvisation. So when the messenger failed to appear in Act II of *La traviata*, he kept his head. A moment earlier he had sung, "Who is there?" and now he answered his own question by singing, "No one." The orchestra doggedly continued playing; the music gave Domingo a moment to marshal his thoughts. He glanced around the set and noticed the table on which Violetta had hastily scrawled her note in the previous scene. Luckily, a stray sheet of paper was still lying on the table. Domingo walked over, picked up the paper, and sang, "Ah! From Violetta!" Then he proceeded with the rest of the scene as it had been written. Years later, Domingo recalled the lesson he learned that night from the missing messenger: "That incident taught me at the very beginning of my career that I had to be prepared for absolutely anything in this business!"

Singing his first leading role made demands on Domingo that he had not expected. The tension of making his debut, the surge of triumph and excitement as the end of the opera drew near, and above all, the tragic beauty of the final scene had a powerful effect on his emotions. In that scene Violetta lies dying in Alfredo's arms and promises to look down on him from heaven while he tries pathetically to convince her that she will not die. Domingo had not yet learned the art of controlling the feelings he was trying to convey to the audience, and he became caught up in the pathos of Violetta's death. To his amazement he found tears streaming down his face. Fortunately, his emotion did not interfere with his singing, and he was able to complete the performance.

Domingo's performance on that nerve-racking night in Monterrey in 1961 was more than simply a creditable debut by a competent and resourceful young singer. It was the beginning of a remarkable career that has made Domingo one of the best-known

Domingo singing the role of Cavaradossi in Giacomo Puccini's opera Tosca. *As a young singer, Domingo concentrated on operas that were not overly taxing to the voice, such as* Tosca *and* La traviata; *in later years he greatly expanded his repertoire and was not afraid to take risks.*

and most admired singers of the 20th century. By 1971, 10 years after his first performance, Domingo had appeared in leading roles at all of the world's leading opera houses and had performed more than 700 times in all. In 1981, to mark his 20th anniversary, he sang in 70 performances of 17 different operas in 21 cities on 4 continents. By this time many people were calling him the world's finest operatic tenor.

Domingo did not confine himself to opera, however; through recordings and concerts he reached an audience of millions with ballads, Christmas songs, zarzuela music, dance tunes, and other forms of popular music. And by 1991, with nearly 200 recordings and a 30-year total of more than 2,000 performances in 90 different operas to his credit, Domingo had established himself as one of the most gifted, versatile, and hardworking singers of all time.

A landscape in the mountainous region of northern Spain, from which Domingo traces part of his ancestry. Northerners are often said to be stubborn and determined, traits that Domingo always considered useful for a performer.

CHAPTER TWO

A Son of Spain

Plácido Domingo was born in Madrid, Spain, on January 21, 1941. Although his later career was to turn him into a globe-trotter, the early years of his life were spent in Spain, where he grew up surrounded by the sights and sounds of his parents' careers in the musical theater. Theater and family were thus intertwined for him from the start. "I cannot remember a time," he wrote in his 1983 autobiography, *My First Forty Years*, "when the stage was not an important part of my existence."

Domingo's grandparents all died either before he was born or when he was a baby, but as he grew up, he heard many stories about them. All of them came from regions in the northern and eastern parts of Spain. The Spanish are very conscious of regional identity; the people who live in each part of the country take great pride in the qualities that are thought to be unique to their region. So one of the first things Domingo learned about his family was its regional origins.

Domingo's paternal grandmother came from Catalonia. She married a man from the neighboring region of Aragon and went to live with him in the Aragonese city of Zaragoza, where he owned a restaurant. After her husband died, she took over the restaurant, which then came to be called La Viuda de Domingo (The Widow of Domingo). Writing of this grandmother, Domingo reported, "She was a woman of incredibly strong character who succeeded in raising her children and in running an establishment frequented by a not always polite clientele: in those days it was more a tavern than a restaurant. For a woman of her generation she was remarkably independent and even drove her own car as early as 1918. Her generosity was well known in the town: once she bought a winning lottery ticket and shared her prize money with her employees."

Domingo's father, Plácido, Sr., was the oldest child in his family. After his father's death, which occurred when he was only 10 years old, he pitched in to help his mother run La Viuda de Domingo. At the same time, the young man developed an interest in music. He studied violin and began to play with orchestras in and around Zaragoza. He also began singing baritone parts in zarzuelas, because the zarzuela tradition gives the larger and more important parts to baritones. In opera, by contrast, the leading role is almost always sung by tenors.

Some listeners thought that Plácido, Sr.'s rather high-pitched baritone voice might really be a heldentenor, a voice that is lower in pitch than most tenors but higher than most baritones—just the type of voice that is required for certain German operas, especially those of Richard Wagner. He was offered an opportunity to study and perform opera in Germany, but he had to turn it down because it would have meant leaving his mother to run the restaurant without his help. "He was devoted to his family," Domingo explained, "and did not want to wander far from home."

In 1940, when Plácido, Sr., was 33 years old, he found himself starring in a zarzuela called *Sor Navarra*, written by a friend of his, composer Federico Moreno Torroba. Singing the leading female role opposite him was a 22-year-old soprano named Pepita Embil.

Embil was a Basque, from the region of northern Spain that lies along the mountainous border with France. She was born in Guetaria, a small fishing village on the Bay of Biscay. Guetaria is noted for having been the birthplace of Juan Sebastián Elcano, the 16th-century navigator who commanded the first ship to sail completely around the world. Because of its picturesque beauty and its historical association with Elcano, Guetaria has been declared a national monument. In more recent years, Domingo noted proudly, the village also prided itself on being the birthplace of his mother, the Queen of Zarzuela, Pepita Embil.

Domingo claims that his combined Basque and Aragonese heritage gave him a certain firmness of character. "Both the Basques and the Aragonese are said to be stubborn, hardheaded," he wrote in his autobiography. "There is a characteristic story about an Aragonese who tells his friends that he can bang a nail into the wall using his head as a hammer. He sets to work and manages to drive it in an inch or two but no further. Why? There is a Basque on the other side of the wall using *his* head to keep the nail from coming through. This is a useful heritage for anyone who makes his career in the performing arts." Domingo points out that Basques are also "known for their love of singing." Pepita Embil was exposed to music and singing early in life. Her father, a church organist, loved to play piano versions of opera; her uncle, a priest who favored a dramatic delivery of the Mass, used to do voice exercises before beginning the liturgy. From her father she acquired familiarity with operatic music; from her uncle, a sense of theater.

Embil started singing when she was young, and the quality of her voice was immediately recognized. Soon she was performing as a soloist with a chorus in the city of San Sebastián, 20 miles from Guetaria. The chorus was well known and made appearances in many cities, so that by the time she was 18, Embil had sung in London and Paris. She remained in Paris for a while to take voice lessons. When she returned, she appeared in a Spanish opera at the Teatro del Liceo in Barcelona, which was Spain's leading opera house at that time. She was ready to launch a career as an operatic soprano.

Embil found it impossible, however, to resist the lure of zarzuela, which is more popular in Spain than classic opera and reaches a wider audience. At the beginning of 1940 she agreed to perform the soprano role in Moreno Torroba's zarzuela *Sor Navarra*, which also starred Plácido Domingo, Sr. During the production, she and Domingo fell in love, and after three months of singing love songs to one another in zarzuela, they decided to

The Gran Via, one of Madrid's main avenues, during the earlier part of the 20th century. During Domingo's childhood in Madrid, his parents were often away on tour; fortunately, he and his sister were surrounded by a loving circle of uncles and aunts.

marry. Embil continued to perform while carrying her first child, who would be named Plácido, Jr.; in fact, she went into labor while still in the theater and had to be brought home in order to give birth. At the time, the Domingos lived on Calle Ibiza (Ibiza Street) in the Barrio de Salamanca. Their apartment house is now adorned with a plaque that proclaims, Plácido Domingo Was Born Here. His sister, Mari Pepa, was born in the same building in September 1942.

Domingo's parents continued to sing together throughout his childhood. When they were first married, they had agreed that Embil would take six months away from zarzuela in order to learn several of the best-known opera roles so that she could accept a contract offer from the Teatro del Liceo. But by this time she had begun to emerge as a star of zarzuela. Composers wrote new works especially for her. She enjoyed the success and security she had found in zarzuela and decided to devote herself to that genre. She was rewarded with great popularity, but Domingo now re-flects that although his parents were extremely proud of their accomplishments in zarzuela, each of them could very likely have made a career in opera. "Two great opera talents were wasted," he once lamented.

Zarzuela provided Domingo's parents with popular success and a measure of financial security, but a life in zarzuela demanded hard work. The Domingos were expected to perform every night during the week, twice on Saturday, and two or three times on Sunday. They traveled a great deal, performing throughout Spain and elsewhere. They would perform each zarzuela as many as 200 times in a row and then immediately move on to the next one. Such a schedule contained serious hazards. During one tour, Domingo's father caught a cold; he continued to sing, and the strain damaged his voice forever. After that, Plácido, Sr., was forced to take roles that required little singing. Domingo learned from his father's experience to safeguard his voice—to take precautions against catching colds and to cancel performances, if necessary, when his throat was under strain. As a result, he has been remarkably successful among opera singers in retaining the quality of his singing voice over a long career.

Despite his parents' frequent absences on performance tours, Domingo's childhood was a warm and happy one. He and his sister were surrounded by a close-knit group of uncles, aunts, and cousins—led by Embil's sister Agustina—who looked after the children when the elder Domingos were on tour. The situation was made more difficult by World War II, which raged throughout Europe and the Pacific from 1939 to 1945. Although Spain remained neutral in that conflict, the nation suffered a severe shortage of foodstuffs, especially white bread and sugar. Domingo recalls that whenever his parents went on tour they would look for bread and sugar to take home for the children.

When the Domingos were performing in Madrid, Plácido, Jr., was able to attend some of his parents' performances. He recalled that he was impressed by the sight of his father in a tuxedo and beard singing in the classic zarzuela *La Gran Via.* He also recalled that his parents' theatrical occupation added color to the Christmas holidays: "Christmas Eve is called Noche Buena in Spain, and it seems to me that my sister and I never really slept on a Noche Buena. There was a tremendous, happy party each year, with all the family and many friends participating. Since my parents were theatre people, there would always be a masquerade—improvised rather than organized. For example, we would be eating when someone would unexpectedly appear at the door, masked and in costume."

For the children, the high point of the holiday season was Epiphany, January 6, which is called Three Kings Day in Spain. On that date Spanish children receive their gifts, which are said to be delivered by the biblical Three Kings instead of by Santa Claus, as in some other countries. Plácido, Jr., and Mari Pepa would write letters to the Three Kings telling what gifts they wanted. Before going to bed on the eve of Three Kings Day, they would set out meals for the kings and pitchers of water for their mounts—a

A family of Spanish refugees crosses into France in 1939, in the brief period between the end of the Spanish civil war and the beginning of World War II. Despite the hardships that Spain endured during the early 1940s, the elder Domingos managed to provide a secure and happy home for Plácido, Jr., and Mari Pepa.

horse, a camel, and an elephant. In the morning the meals would be eaten, the pitchers would be empty, and the gifts would be accompanied by a letter from the Three Kings warning the children to be good during the coming year. "It was all magical," Domingo wrote. "The special feeling of wonderment for things theatrical became part of me very early."

Other theatrical episodes in Domingo's early life involved Guetaria, his mother's home village. Every summer, the family would visit Guetaria, where the mayor would enact a little pageant about Elcano's return from his voyage around the world. This drama was followed by a celebration. One summer, when Plácido, Jr., was five or six years old, the festival included a visit by a traveling circus. The ringmaster asked for a volunteer to play the big bass drum, and to the astonishment of his sister and his aunt Agustina, Plácido, Jr., stepped forward from the crowd. "That was my artistic debut," he later asserted.

In 1946, the composer Federico Moreno Torroba once again had a hand in shaping the destiny of the Domingo family. He formed a new zarzuela company and planned a tour of performances in Puerto Rico, Mexico, and Cuba. Domingo's parents were part of the company, and Domingo and his sister were left in the care of Aunt Agustina.

The Domingos had never been away from home for so long before, and Plácido, Jr., was very unhappy during the extended separation. At this time the family moved to a new apartment two blocks away, and Plácido, Jr., started school. His school, the Colegio Ibérico, was on the same street as his new home. At the end of the street was an entrance to Madrid's magnificent public park, the Retiro, which contains a zoo, a lake, lush gardens, and ample spaces where children can play. Plácido, Jr., was comforted by the routine he soon established, moving between home, school, and the Retiro.

While Plácido, Jr., was adjusting to a new phase in his life, his parents were embarking on an adventure of their own. The zarzuela tour was a great success. After the tour ended in Cuba, Plácido, Sr., and Embil decided to take a vacation in Mexico before returning to Spain. They had liked Mexico very much when they performed there, and they had been well received by the Mexican public. During their holiday, they grew even more attached to the country and the people. They agreed to stay an extra week, and then another. The weeks stretched into months, and the Domingos forgot about returning to Spain. Instead, they resolved to form their own zarzuela company in Mexico City, with Plácido, Sr., as the manager and Embil as the star soprano. They decided that they would send for the children once they had established themselves and were certain that they would all be able to make a life in Mexico.

It took two years, but the Domingos succeeded in creating their zarzuela company and establishing themselves securely in Mexico. At that point they were ready to send for the children. In December 1948, Plácido, Jr., Mari Pepa, and Aunt Agustina boarded a ship called the *Marqués de Comillas* at the Spanish port of Bilbao for their journey to Mexico. Domingo recalls that the last thing he did before leaving Spain was to drink an *horchata*, an almond-flavored drink of which he was especially fond. It would be 17 years before he would return to Spain and taste another horchata.

The Three Kings, *depicted here by the 16th-century Flemish painter Quentin Massys, take the place of Santa Claus in Spanish-speaking countries. Although the Domingo children were on a ship bound for Mexico on Three Kings Day in 1949, the legendary kings somehow managed to deliver their presents.*

CHAPTER THREE

New Directions

Nothing could be more beautiful for two small children than a month-long boat trip," observed Domingo of the voyage that took him from Spain to his new home in Mexico. He and Mari Pepa, along with the 20 or so other children on the ship, enjoyed running around on the top deck, eating in the dining hall, and watching movies every night—and they were relieved to discover, on January 6, that the Three Kings had managed to find their ship and deliver their gifts in the middle of the ocean.

Upon arriving in the New World, the *Marqués de Comillas* made stops in Curaçao, Venezuela, and Puerto Rico. The next stop was Cuba, where the intense heat and the sights and sounds of the harbor made a powerful impression on young Plácido during the three days the ship spent in Havana. Then, on January 18, 1949, three days before Plácido's eighth birthday, the ship reached the Mexican port of Veracruz. The ship could not dock right away; it had to wait at anchor in the harbor for a day while the authorities checked the passengers' papers. But the elder Domingos, eager to see their children after the long separation, hired a motorboat and came out to the ship for an emotional reunion.

The Domingo family, including Aunt Agustina, drove from Veracruz to Mexico City, where Plácido, Sr., and Embil were in the midst of a busy season of zarzuela. They were also having an apartment prepared behind a shop where Embil planned to sell babies' clothing imported from Spain. Just as in Spain, however, the senior Domingos were frequently absent on tour, and Aunt Agustina looked after the children during these absences. Plácido, Jr., and Mari Pepa loved their aunt Agustina, but at times they found her guardianship rather strict.

The children had arrived in the middle of the school year, and their parents decided to enroll them for the rest of that year in an American-run institution called the Windsor School. The school's program included an English class, but Plácido, Jr., did not learn English in the few months he spent at Windsor. At the beginning of the next school year he was enrolled in the Instituto México, a Mexican academy for boys.

Plácido had a wonderful time at the Instituto México—he loved soccer, and the school's soccer team, of which he was a member, played two games a day. His teacher indulged the soccer players, allowing them to wear their soccer uniforms underneath their regular clothes and then strip down during the final minutes of class; this way they were able to rush outside and begin playing as soon as the bell rang. Domingo later estimated that during his school years he played soccer for about two and a half hours each day.

According to Domingo, "The two standard ambitions of Spanish boys are to be soccer goalkeepers and to be bullfighters." He fulfilled one ambition by taking the position of goalkeeper on the school team. One day, when he was 14 years old, he attempted to fulfill the other ambition: He went with some friends to a *tientas*, or training ring, to try his luck as a bullfighter. "The bull I was given to fight was only the size of a small dog," he recalled, "despite which

I was afraid that I would be hurt and that my parents might find out. It chased me and flung me to the ground, and I went back to being a goalkeeper."

Soccer was not young Plácido's only passion. He had grown up listening to his mother and father sing, and he enjoyed singing around the house. He later claimed that as a child he had "a nice voice, nothing special." Nevertheless, when he was eight years old, his parents entered him in a singing and dancing contest for children, organized by a Spanish musical company performing in Mexico. Young Plácido—who recalled his appearance on the occasion as "very fat and dressed in short pants"—sang a song and won first prize, consisting of a soccer ball and some books. He promptly gave the prize away to another child, but he remained proud of having won the competition, which he designated his "debut in the Western Hemisphere."

During his years at the Instituto México, Plácido always volunteered whenever a singer was needed for a school assembly or program. He was eager to perform, but his repertoire was limited to a single song, the popular Mexican ballad "Granada." His fellow students heard him sing that song so many times that they nicknamed him El Granado.

Plácido's musical education had two aspects, one informal and the other formal. The informal training was the experience he

A view of the harbor of Veracruz, Mexico. Eager to see their children after a two-year absence, the elder Domingos rented a motorboat and met their ship as it lay at anchor. "The experience of seeing our parents again was overwhelming for both my sister and myself," Domingo later recalled.

gained as an observer of and a participant in his parents' zarzuela company. Not only did Plácido and Mari Pepa attend many performances, but from time to time, when children were needed in a production, they took the parts. "I began to learn the basics of theatrical practice from the time I was small," Domingo recalled. "I attended orchestra and stage rehearsals, watched the set and costume designers at work, and placed the music on the orchestra's music stands." He learned other lessons as well, including "the harsher aspects of the theatre world." Because his parents were not merely performers but also owners and managers of the company, they had to worry about the many business details that accompanied each production. He would often see them peering out at the auditorium before the curtain went up, hoping that the house would be full and the performance a good one. "I have never forgotten either that insecure feeling or the realization that whatever happened, they were artists and had to give their best," he later said. The sense of responsibility to the audience that distinguished Domingo's own career as a performer was instilled by years of exposure to his parents' professionalism and dedication.

His formal music education began when he was eight years old. At that time, he and Mari Pepa began taking piano lessons from a teacher named Manuel Barajas. The two nephews of Esperanza Vázquez's, a family friend, took lessons from Barajas at the same time. The lessons were given twice a week after school, and Vázquez and Aunt Agustina generally came to Barajas's home to pick up the pupils. If the lessons had not gone well, Barajas would shout down the stairwell, "Aunts, upstairs!" The aunts would come up and listen to the teacher berate the pupil who had performed poorly.

Young Plácido showed real ability at the piano, which greatly pleased his mother and father. "My parents wanted me to be a pianist; they didn't want me to go on the stage," he recalled. "They saw the world in terms of zarzuela and how difficult it was, and they wanted to spare me that." The question of Plácido, Jr.'s music future assumed greater urgency when he was 14 years old. That year, Manuel Barajas became ill and died, and the elder Domingos had to decide what form of music education was now best for their son. By this time he had demonstrated enough skill at the keyboard to occasionally play at rehearsals and even for some performances of the zarzuela company. The Domingos decided that Plácido's piano training should continue, with the goal of preparing him for a career as a professional musician. Instead of finding him another piano teacher, however, they enrolled him at the National Conservatory of Music in Mexico City. They believed that conservatory training would give their son a thorough, well-rounded music education.

A conservatory is a special school devoted to the development of musicians, including instrumentalists, conductors, singers, and composers. Young Plácido's primary studies at the conservatory were in piano, but he was also required to study a variety of other music subjects as well as such academic subjects as Spanish, history, literature, and mathematics.

Plácido's enthusiasm for the piano declined at the conservatory, perhaps because the method of teaching was quite different from what he had become used to with Barajas. "Instead of a concentrated hour every three or four days, as I had been accustomed to having with my private teacher, I now had twenty minutes

A view of the Metropolitan Cathedral and the Plaza de la Constitución in Mexico City. Domingo began his music studies in Mexico with the idea of becoming a pianist, but the death of his first piano teacher caused him to shift his main interest to singing.

here and twenty minutes there," he recalled. "My mind blocked and I lost interest, although I did receive training in other important skills and subjects."

These subjects included singing, harmony, and the basics of composition, or writing music. In addition to his formal studies, Plácido benefited from being surrounded by musical excellence. The National Conservatory numbered several outstanding musicians on its faculty. Among them were Carlos Chávez, a noted composer and conductor, and Julián Carrillo, who wrote piano music. The staff also included singing teachers and voice coaches, and they sparked Domingo's first interest in opera. "Before long I noticed the singers from the National Opera coming to the conservatory for lessons or coaching sessions, and my curiosity was aroused," he said. "I observed several teachers' classes; the world of opera slowly began to fascinate me, although I had not then even begun to sing zarzuela with my parents."

Thrown together with other young people who were dedicating themselves to a life in music, young Plácido forged new friendships at the conservatory. One friend was Eduardo Mata, who became a well-known conductor. Mata and Domingo used to find excuses to get out of their biology and math classes so that they could play four-handed piano—piano pieces written for two players. They also worked at their own compositions and together wrote a piece of music that they called Sinfonietta no. 1 in C. Later, when Mata was taking a class in conducting, Domingo sat in on the class as an observer and picked up some knowledge of conducting, which he was to put to good use in his own music career.

Another new friend was Pepe Esteva, who, like Plácido, came from a musical family: His mother played the harp, his sister played the guitar, and his brother was a violinist and conductor. Every Monday evening, the Esteva family held informal music parties for as few as 5 or as many as 20 people, and Domingo became a regular at these sessions. Everyone brought food from home, and Esteva's mother brewed pot after pot of coffee. The gatherings began at eight-thirty or nine and sometimes lasted until two or three in the morning. Plácido sang from time to time, but he was most often asked to play the piano while someone else sang or performed on another instrument. He generally showed up with a huge stack of music under his arm—the accompaniments for everyone else's selections. He worked his way through many violin and piano sonatas with Esteva's brother, but above all he accompanied the singers. It was not unusual on these occasions for leading singers from the National Opera to put in an appearance. Plácido was impressed by their singing, and he also enjoyed listening to their chitchat about the opera productions in which they appeared. At this time opera still seemed a remote and glamorous world to the young pianist.

The Estevas' weekly music parties turned out to be an important part of Domingo's education. "I developed as a musician more through those weekly sessions than through any other activity of my early years," he later wrote. "The amount of repertoire I devoured was impressive, and the experience taught me when and how to lead, when and how to follow, and a great deal about different musical styles and different types of voices. My participation in those sessions went on for at least three years; I found them so instructive and enjoyable that I look back on them with love and regret. I wish I had time today for more informal music making."

The exterior of Mexico City's main bullring, where thousands of spectators regularly gather to watch bullfights. At the age of 14, Domingo dreamed of becoming a bullfighter; however, an encounter with a small but angry bull convinced him that he ought to stick to music.

Domingo later believed that the death of Manuel Barajas, followed as it was by the beginning of his own studies at the National Conservatory of Music, was a turning point in his life. "If Barajas had lived," he wrote in his autobiography, "I would most likely have tried to become a concert pianist; and although I had great facility at the piano and could sight-read well and play in a naturally musical way, I doubt that I could ever have become an outstanding keyboard artist." His entry into the conservatory changed the musical direction of Domingo's life by exposing him to opera and symphonic music and by teaching him the basics of writing and conducting music. It also brought an upheaval in his family life, one that was to have profound and long-lasting consequences.

"When I entered the conservatory," Domingo recalled, "I was a boy, with nothing in my head except soccer and the piano." His classes at the Instituto México had been for boys only, but at the National Conservatory they included girls. Classes and practice sessions often lasted into the evening, giving the students opportunities to spend time with one another instead of going straight home at the end of the day. Young Plácido became very interested in some of the girls at school, and eventually he began dating one girl in particular. She was a piano student and was two years older than he. "By this time," he remembered, "I was making my first attempts at singing, and she would accompany me at the piano."

Plácido had no idea how to cope with the feelings that this first romance aroused. He had received little guidance in emotional or sexual matters from his father, who was often away from home and was very busy with the zarzuela company even when he was at home. As his relationship with his girlfriend progressed, Plácido became convinced that they were deeply in love and should get married. Like many teenagers, he was restless, eager to become an adult, and ready to rebel against authority—in his case, against his aunt's strictness. All of these factors urged the young man to make a dramatic decision. "At the age of sixteen—and barely sixteen at that—I made up my mind to leave home and live with this girl," he recalled.

The two young people ran away, hiding at the home of one of the girl's brothers. Then they secretly got married. By this time the elder Domingos, who had been in Europe, had learned what had happened. They rushed back to Mexico City, found their son, and took him home, determined that the episode would end there. But Plácido convinced his father to let him visit his new wife, and together they went to see her at her parents' house. "When it was time to leave," Domingo recalled, "I said to my father, 'Please, I feel I have to stay.'" Although Plácido, Sr., was not at all pleased with this turn of events, he gave in to his son's wishes. The young couple found an apartment. She became pregnant, and a son, whom they named José, was born in June 1958, when Plácido was 17 years old.

The marriage failed soon after it had begun. "It did not take long for us to realize that the situation was completely impossible," Domingo later reflected. "We were so young, and we had no experience of life, of ourselves." He and his wife separated less than a year after they were married, and their divorce became final a year after their separation.

Domingo recalled the experience of marriage, fatherhood, and divorce as "terribly harrowing" for a teenage boy. But he added, "In one sense, getting married accelerated my career, because it meant that I had to find work, had to do anything to support my wife, our child, and myself."

Domingo's formal education came to an end with his marriage. He dropped out of the National Conservatory and became a sort of musical odd-job man, taking on all kinds of work. Looking back, Domingo was convinced that his departure from the conservatory, abrupt though it was, probably had a good effect on his career: "Had I remained at the conservatory, I might have become what we call a 'conservatory rat'—someone who learns to do everything proficiently but never develops into a real performer. Leaving it opened the way to new experiences and made me independent."

Those new experiences were soon to include opera, but first Domingo had to learn that independence sometimes meant simply working hard to make a living.

Plácido Domingo at the beginning of his operatic career. Though he had always considered himself a baritone, the directors of the National Opera of Mexico signed him to sing tenor roles; this allowed him to be the leading man in most operas.

CHAPTER FOUR

The World of Opera

Domingo's first job was to play piano as his mother's accompanist when she sang in a concert in the city of Mérida, in Mexico's Yucatán region. He then began performing with his parents' zarzuela company, occasionally playing piano but more often singing. As his father had done, he sang in a baritone voice and took the leading parts. He realized at this time that he was headed toward a career as a singer, and he believed that his future lay in zarzuela.

Although he never had a singing teacher, Domingo had received a good deal of informal training from his parents. While he was a student at the conservatory, he had paid attention during the voice classes and had sung for several of the teachers, who offered suggestions for improving his technique. He remembers that one teacher concentrated on the mechanics of the voice, explaining to him, for example, what his forehead muscles were doing when he sang. He did not find this information particularly helpful, but he continued to pick up tips on singing technique wherever he could.

Although he had left the conservatory after his marriage, Domingo managed to sit in on voice classes taught by Carlo Morelli, a well-known baritone from Chile. "I was curious about Morelli," Domingo later wrote, "because I knew that many of Mexico's best professional singers went to him for coaching." He found that Morelli concentrated not on mechanical technique but on inter-pretation—the art of looking beyond the notes to unlock mood and meaning in a piece of music. Morelli taught Domingo to search for the emotional and spiritual aspects of each work and to try to convey these to his audience.

Morelli's class was also important to Domingo because it was there, with Morelli's encouragement, that he reached a high note in the tenor vocal range—the high B-flat—for the first time. This is quite an accomplishment for any singer, and especially for one who believed he was a baritone. It so happened that Adolfo López Mateos, the president of Mexico, was visiting the class that day. Domingo was one of four students who performed for him, sing-ing a quartet from the opera *La Bohème*. Domingo was told years later by a member of the class—a girl named Marta Ornelas, who became his second wife—that he screeched those new B-flats at the top of his lungs, showing off for the president.

Despite the B-flats, Domingo continued to sing baritone roles in the zarzuela company. With his parents, he toured all over Mexico and appeared in many popular zarzuelas. He also made his debut as a conductor in *Luisa Fernanda*, by the Domingos' old friend Moreno Torroba. The starring roles that night were sung by his mother and a young baritone named Franco Iglesias, who had made his own singing debut with the Domingos' company eight years earlier. Iglesias was seven years older than Domingo, but the two soon became good friends. Iglesias was to play an important role in Domingo's music career. Among other things, he was one of the first to suggest that Domingo sing as a tenor rather than as a baritone.

Domingo was greatly influenced by the Chilean baritone Carlo Morelli. Morelli taught Domingo how to interpret music and helped him reach the higher notes that eventually enabled him to become a tenor.

Domingo remained a baritone, however, for his next job, singing in musical comedy. Musical comedies, or musicals, as they are often called, differ from zarzuelas in that they usually contain even more spoken dialogue. Essentially, they are plays with songs set into the text, and the songs are likely to be catchy rather than vocally challenging. Even the best-loved operas, those performed again and again over the decades, cannot approach the popular success of musical comedies, especially those that enjoy long runs in New York City's Broadway theaters.

Perhaps the most popular musical of all time has been *My Fair Lady*, in which a snobbish professor, Henry Higgins, wins a bet by turning Eliza Doolittle, a scruffy flower girl, into an elegant lady and then finds to his dismay that he has fallen in love with her. *My Fair Lady*—adapted from George Bernard Shaw's play *Pygmalion*—had broken all box-office records in both London and New York during the late 1950s, and a Spanish-language version was slated to open in Mexico City. Domingo auditioned and was assigned a small role as one of Eliza's father's drinking buddies. Perhaps more important, he was also hired as an assistant conductor and assistant coach for the chorus, which gave him valuable experience.

Although his own singing part was small, Domingo's first stint in musical comedy was rather grueling. "Incredible as it may seem," he recalled, "there was a performance of *My Fair Lady* every day and two on Sundays. We never had a day off. In all, I did 185 performances without interruption." The strain of maintaining such a demanding schedule and the boredom of doing the same things over and over again took a toll on the performers, who resorted to practical jokes to keep their spirits up. Someone performing a scene would be handed a chair to sit on, for example, and the chair would have a broken leg, resulting in unplanned laughs from the audience.

Domingo's role called for him to wear shabby clothes. But toward the end of the play, when Eliza's father decides to get married and become a respectable gent, Domingo had to appear in a tuxedo as part of the chorus. One night while he was changing, he discovered that his fancy dress shoes had been firmly nailed to the floor. He did not have enough time to pry them loose, so he sang in the chorus wearing his tuxedo and a pair of "horrible old clodhoppers," as he remembered them. The management fined the high-spirited performers for each of their pranks, and Domingo's clodhoppers cost him some of his paycheck.

Many of the singers in *My Fair Lady*, including the soprano who sang the leading role of Eliza Doolittle, were aspiring opera singers. Domingo listened with fascination when they talked about their studies and ambitions, but he had no thought of joining them. "I was only beginning to dream about opera at that time," he recalled. "It seemed fantastically remote, especially since I had not even heard many operas."

He spent much of his time with a young singer named Cristina, who was launching a career as a nightclub performer. In order to

Julie Andrews and Rex Harrison (center) in a scene from the original 1956 production of My Fair Lady. *Following its triumphant run on Broadway, the musical was performed around the world; the Mexican version provided Domingo with one of his first professional singing jobs.*

be with her, he started playing in clubs as her accompanist. He also played the piano for a baritone from his parents' company who sang at a cabaret where striptease shows were the main attraction. This experience taught Domingo to remain calm and keep his temper in the face of an unruly audience, because every time the baritone started to sing, the audience began to shout, "Go away! We want the girls!" Domingo recalled, "It was quite an experience to accompany someone in romantic songs while the audience roared, 'Finish already! Shut up!' and much worse. But we both saw the humor of the situation and took it lightly."

When *My Fair Lady* ended its run, Domingo was hired to sing in Franz Lehár's popular operetta *The Merry Widow.* He appeared in more than 170 performances of this work, and he also appeared for a while in a production of a musical detective story called *The Redhead.* But his days in musical comedy and light opera ended in 1959, when Manuel Aguilar, a friend from the National Conservatory, persuaded him to set his sights on an operatic career.

Aguilar arranged an audition for Domingo at the National Opera of Mexico in Mexico City. Domingo studied baritone arias from two operas, and when the important day arrived, he sang them before the auditioning committee. The committee members huddled together for a few moments and then called Domingo forward. They liked his voice, they told him—but they felt he should be a tenor, not a baritone. Did he have any tenor arias to present? Domingo did not know any tenor material, but his experience in sight-reading new music, both at the conservatory and at the Estevas' musical gatherings, now showed its usefulness. He offered to sight-read something and was handed an aria that he had never heard. He tackled it gamely, singing higher notes than he was used to, and he was appalled to hear his voice crack on one of the high notes. But the committee heard the promise in his voice, and they offered him a contract as a tenor with the National Opera on the spot.

"I was amazed and thrilled," Domingo remembered, "especially since the contract was financially decent and I was only eighteen." The contract would not only improve Domingo's income, but it would give him a real chance to see whether he could make it in the fiercely competitive, extremely demanding world of opera. He was also hired to play the piano at rehearsals and coaching sessions, and by doing this he learned a great deal about the operas being performed by the company. At the same time, he

A youthful Domingo hits a high note. When he tried out for the National Opera of Mexico in 1959, Domingo's voice cracked when he reached for an unfamiliar high note in the tenor range; to his surprise, the audition committee ignored the mistake and offered him a contract on the spot.

had to retrain himself to sing as a tenor. He accomplished this on his own, although he did get suggestions from Carlo Morelli at the National Academy and from his friend Franco Iglesias.

The shift from baritone to tenor had momentous consequences for Domingo; it changed the whole shape of his prospective career. As a baritone in zarzuela he had been able to count on having the leading roles. If he had entered opera as a baritone, this would not have been the case. Tenors have the leading, or heroic, parts in most operas. Although much wonderful opera music has been written for the baritone voice, baritones are generally somewhat secondary in opera stories—they play the role of the villain, or perhaps the brother or friend of the hero. As one opera proverb says, "The baritone is the one who *doesn't* get the girl." And in terms of fame and fortune, the leading tenors among male singers—and the leading sopranos among female singers—almost always enjoy the most public acclaim and the highest fees. There is something about the ringing voice of the tenor, soaring to reach the highest notes possible for the male voice, that appeals even to those who do not like opera.

Tenor singing is tremendously stirring and exciting, but it also carries the ever-present possibility that the voice will crack or go flat on the high notes. The showiest and most demanding tenor arias have often been compared to high-wire circus acts, with the audience holding its breath in mingled pleasure and suspense. "The natural male voice is baritone," Domingo has explained. "The tenor voice is unnatural, more exposed. We are always taking risks. And when you crack a note, as we all do because it's human, it is terrible."

The National Opera of Mexico had two distinct seasons—a national season that featured Mexican performers and an international season that brought to Mexico leading performers from around the world. Domingo was hired as a *comprimario*, a singer of small or secondary parts, for the international season. His first role, in September 1959, was a minor one in Verdi's opera *Rigoletto*.

The part may have been small, but excitement in the Domingo household ran high. Domingo's parents used their theatrical connections to have a magnificent costume made for him; he was in danger of outshining the star performers. He had few opportunities to do so that year; during the entire 1959 season, Domingo sang a total of only four performances.

By contrast, the 1960 and 1961 seasons of the National Opera were filled with new and thrilling experiences for Domingo. His first performance in 1960 was in the role of the emperor in Puccini's *Turandot.* He had almost nothing to sing, but he enjoyed wearing the emperor's gorgeous costume. One day during rehearsals, he happened to walk into the hall while the chorus was practicing "Perchè tarda la luna" (Why does the moon delay). Domingo had never heard *Turandot* before, and that chorus suddenly revealed to him the full beauty and majesty of opera, his chosen life's work. "Perhaps if I were to hear them today," he later reflected, "I would notice that the orchestra was playing flat or the chorus was not singing so well, but at that moment the music had the most profound effect on me. It was one of the most moving experiences of my life, the most beautiful thing I had ever heard."

By participating in the National Opera's international season, Domingo occasionally was privileged to share the stage with singers of worldwide renown. Several times he sang in productions that starred the Italian tenor Giuseppe di Stefano. One of the world's leading singers in the years following World War II, di Stefano was often paired with the famed soprano Maria Callas, and the two made many classic recordings together. Domingo later asserted that di Stefano was the most impressive tenor he had ever heard: "The beauty, warmth, and passion of his voice, the excellence of his phrasing, and, above all, his masterly delivery of every word were a great inspiration to me."

This brilliant artist was not without his share of vanity, however. In August 1961, di Stefano was singing the part of Alfredo in the National Opera's Mexico City production of *La traviata*—the same

Giuseppe di Stefano, one of the leading tenors of the post–World War II era, poses for a photo in the lobby of the old Metropolitan Opera House in New York City. When he sang with the National Opera of Mexico during the early 1960s, di Stefano impressed Domingo with both his artistry and his ego.

part in which Domingo had made his own leading-role debut in Monterrey just a few months earlier. Domingo had a much smaller part in the Mexico City production, and the part of Giorgio Germont, Alfredo's father, was sung by a baritone named Manuel Ausensi. One night Ausensi gave such a brilliant and heartfelt rendering of the aria in which he begs Violetta to release Alfredo that the audience erupted into cheers and demanded an encore. Ausensi and the orchestra obliged. This upset di Stefano, who felt that Ausensi had stolen his limelight. Di Stefano threatened not to go back onstage for the rest of the opera.

There was an agitated backstage conference, and finally one of the managers said, "Well, Mr. di Stefano, if you refuse to go out, this Domingo boy will have to take over for you. Fortunately he made his debut as Alfredo in Monterrey a few months ago." Di Stefano thereupon agreed to complete the performance, and Domingo missed the opportunity to step in for one of the premier tenors of the day. Just such an opportunity, however, was to come his way some years later in New York City.

In the meantime, Domingo got on with the business of earning a living. The National Opera did not provide a full-time job; the season was short, and he appeared in only a handful of productions. In 1960 he sang only six times. In 1961 he sang 22 times, including his leading-role debut as Alfredo and his first performance as Cavaradossi, the painter and revolutionary who is the leading male character in Puccini's *Tosca*.

His final appearances of 1961 were in Dallas, Texas, where he had a small part in the Dallas Civic Opera's production of Gaetano Donizetti's *Lucia di Lammermoor*. This production was important to Domingo for two reasons: It was his debut in the United States, and it enabled him to sing for the first time with Joan Sutherland, who was soon recognized as one of the great opera singers of all time. Above all, he was impressed during his visit by the apparent wealth of the United States. "Although I did not then understand English," he remembered, "I was amazed by what I saw on television—especially on the quiz shows, where money, furs, and cars were given away." He also liked the friendliness of the American managers, stagehands, and singers, who seemed to go out of their way to make him feel comfortable.

During his first trip to the United States, Domingo had a chance to appear with the great Australian soprano Joan Sutherland, shown here in a performance during the early 1960s. The affluence of American society and the friendliness of the people made a deep impression on the young Spaniard.

In the spring of 1962 he sang for American audiences in New Orleans, Louisiana, and in Tampa, Florida, where for the first time he had the main tenor part in Puccini's *Madama Butterfly*, one of the best-known and best-loved of all operas, the story of a Japanese woman who falls in love with an American naval officer and kills herself in despair when she learns that he has abandoned her. That same season he took the leading tenor part in *Lucia di Lammermoor* in a production in Fort Worth, Texas; the soprano was Lily Pons, a legendary singer who at age 58 was appearing in her final *Lucia*. Domingo liked the thought that when he shared the stage with Pons, who 30 years earlier had sung with the most famous tenors of the previous generation, he became part of a living operatic tradition that linked the singers of the past with those of the present and future.

Between opera productions, Domingo took any job he could find. For a while he played piano for a touring ballet company that could not afford an orchestra. It was not a bad job, but Domingo, always susceptible to female beauty, was occasionally distracted by the sight of 20 or 25 young women in ballet costumes pirouetting around the stage while he played. He also found work in Mexico's recording industry, preparing arrangements of American pop tunes for several of Mexico's best-known popular singers. From time to time he worked in zarzuela, either singing or coaching.

Around this time, the Mexican broadcasting network introduced a new television channel devoted to cultural programs. Domingo managed to get a show of his own on this station. It was a music program in which he played piano accompaniment for singers who performed songs from opera, zarzuela, and musical comedy. The biggest challenge was to find performers for the show, and Domingo called upon friends from the National Conservatory and the National Opera to take part. Once he had the performers lined up, Domingo was responsible for all the other tasks associated with a television broadcast. He chose the pieces to be performed and provided the arrangements and sheet music; he arranged for costumes, wigs, makeup, and props, some of which he was able to borrow from his parents' zarzuela company; and at showtime he had to play the piano and sometimes sing.

Producing this television show was a good introduction to the perils of working live on camera. During one program, when a soprano and a baritone were singing a duet, the baritone's false beard came unstuck and dangled from his chin; Domingo made furious gestures from his seat at the piano, but the poor baritone stared back uncomprehendingly until the beard fell off. On another occasion a tenor lost half of his false mustache, which Domingo considered "worse than losing a whole beard."

The music program was not Domingo's only television work. He and his girlfriend, Cristina, the nightclub singer, took an acting class together, and soon thereafter they took part in a drama series on the cultural television channel. The show consisted of live broadcasts of works by such playwrights as Luigi Pirandello, Federico García Lorca, and Anton Chekhov. Although Domingo took only minor roles in these nonmusical productions, he felt that the experience was good training for him, strengthening his acting ability—something that is often glaringly lacking in opera performers. Throughout his own career, Domingo has been admired by critics and audiences alike for the way he acts each role onstage instead of merely singing it, and he has performed better in movies than any other major opera star.

In addition to gaining experience in a variety of fields, Domingo also embarked on a new romance. His divorce had become final in 1959, and by 1961 his relationship with Cristina had begun to cool off. He became interested in another young woman, one he had known from his days at the conservatory. She was also a singer, and like Domingo, she was at the start of a career in opera. She was, in fact, somewhat more advanced in her career than he was in his. Her name was Marta Ornelas.

Plácido Domingo and Mirella Freni perform a duet in Madama Butterfly. *The part of Lieutenant Pinkerton, the American officer who woos and then abandons a Japanese woman, was Domingo's first leading role in a U.S. production.*

Domingo and Ornelas had not shown much interest in each other when they first met. "Marta was part of the intellectual crowd," Domingo later explained. "I was this fellow who worked in my parents' company, who played the piano in a nightclub while a dancer took her clothes off, who'd had a child and been divorced, who was singing in musical comedies, arranging choral parts for record companies, and producing a musical variety show on TV. I thought she looked down on me. I found out later she was dying to be asked to appear on my show." It was not until Domingo joined the National Opera, where Ornelas was already established as a soprano, that they began to feel comfortable with each other.

Domingo and Ornelas began spending time together when they appeared in the same production in May 1961, and during the next year they made a point of seeing each other or talking on the telephone every day. Their growing romance encountered some opposition at first. Ornelas's mother did not feel that Domingo was quite good enough for her daughter. In order to win over Mrs. Ornelas, Domingo resorted to a Spanish musical tradition—the serenade. He would go to a plaza and hire a mariachi band—the musicians were always surprised when he told them that he, not they, would be doing the singing. Then he would lead them to the street where the Ornelases lived and start serenading beneath the third-floor windows, making sure to include the songs of Mrs. Ornelas's favorite singer, the Mexican balladeer Jorge Negrete. The midnight serenades were not always welcomed by the neighbors, who finally called the police. But when the police arrived, they said to the complainers, "What are you protesting about? You're getting a beautiful performance, free, by a member of the National Opera."

Not all of the young couple's meetings were so fanciful. They spent a lot of time helping each other with voice exercises and practicing new parts together. Ornelas, who had been singing longer than Domingo and who had had formal voice training, gave him tips and encouragement. She was in a position to do so because she was achieving considerable success. After performing in Wolfgang Amadeus Mozart's *Le nozze di Figaro* (The Marriage of Figaro) in 1962, she won an award as the best Mexican singer of the year. At this time, Domingo was just starting to be viewed as a serious singer and was very much in her shadow.

That year, when the National Opera's season ended, Ornelas, Domingo, and Domingo's baritone friend Franco Iglesias formed their own three-member opera company and went on tour. They

Domingo in the leading male role in Andrea Chénier, *which he performed often in Mexico. Following the 1962 season, Domingo went on tour with soprano Marta Ornelas, who was soon to be his wife, and baritone Franco Iglesias.*

used a simple set that included a piano. Domingo sat at the piano and played while Ornelas and Iglesias sang two brief operas, and then the three singers presented a variety of arias and duets. Their bookings were arranged by agents in Mexico City, who created a whirlwind schedule that had the three singers traveling all over Mexico, performing every night, sleeping on buses, and living out of their suitcases.

The tour was a success, and Domingo was particularly pleased that Ornelas's parents had allowed her to travel with him. He decided that the time had come to propose marriage. Ornelas accepted and soon won her parents' approval. The wedding took place on August 1, 1962, and was followed by a honeymoon in Acapulco.

The remainder of that year was a hectic one for the newlyweds. There were further performances of their small touring opera group, and in addition, both of them sang in National Opera productions. Domingo also made four appearances in New Orleans and elsewhere in the United States; it was at this time that he sang with Lily Pons in Fort Worth. He also appeared in four television broadcasts of zarzuelas and operettas sponsored by the Max Factor cosmetics company; Ornelas, Iglesias, and Domingo's parents also took part in the series.

Producers and directors were realizing that Domingo was the ideal leading man for such productions. Now 21 years old, he stood 6 feet 2 inches tall; even though his shoulders were a bit rounded and he tended to gain weight easily, he was an impressive and handsome young man. In addition, he possessed a great deal of stage experience, a fair amount of acting ability, and a voice that was beginning to show the richness of maturity.

Although he had made considerable progress since his first opera audition in 1959, Domingo was now looking for a way to propel his career forward. He was eager to perform more often, to take more leading parts, to earn a larger income so that he and Ornelas could think about raising a family, and perhaps even to start making an international name for himself. He had been overjoyed to hear, on the day before his wedding, that he had won a brand-new music scholarship. He thought about using the money to pay for lessons in Italy or New York, but just then he learned that the Hebrew National Opera in Tel Aviv, Israel, was looking for a soprano, a tenor, and a baritone. Domingo, Ornelas, and Iglesias sent sample tapes to Tel Aviv, and all three were offered work there for six months, to start at the end of 1962.

Domingo was delighted by the offer. Without hesitation he decided to go to Tel Aviv as a performer rather than to New York or Italy as a student. He knew that he had much to learn before he could succeed as an opera singer, but he preferred to learn by doing rather than by studying. He was less delighted, however, when he found that he was no longer eligible for his scholarship, on the grounds that he had accepted work as a professional singer. He also found out that the £1,000 per month offered in the opera contract were Israeli pounds, not British ones; this meant that he and Ornelas together would be earning only the equivalent of $333 each month. Their contract indicated that they would be asked to sing as many as 10 times a month—and most established singers feel that 4 to 6 performances per month is a full schedule. Once Domingo and Ornelas had examined their contracts closely, they discovered that they would earn about $16.65 per performance in Tel Aviv.

Despite these drawbacks, Domingo, Ornelas, and Iglesias decided to go ahead with the Tel Aviv venture. It was a chance for them to see a bit of the world while gaining valuable experience—and perhaps a chance to attract the attention of European opera producers.

The trio set off for Israel in December 1962. For Domingo, the months ahead were to be a prolonged test that would bring him to full maturity as a singer.

Domingo performs the title role in Argentine composer Alberto Ginastera's
Don Rodrigo. *Starring in the opera's 1966 world premiere in New York
City was a special thrill for Domingo because he was singing in Spanish
and introducing the work of a living Hispanic composer.*

CHAPTER FIVE

A Decade of Firsts

The Domingos arrived in Tel Aviv a few days before Christmas, and their mood was far from cheery. They had had to make a long train trip across the United States in order to catch a plane in New York; the big trunk containing all their costumes had first been mistakenly unloaded in St. Louis and then stranded in New York by a dockworkers strike; and for the first time they would have to spend the holidays away from their families. On December 29, Domingo made his debut in Israel, singing the lead tenor role of Rodolfo in Puccini's *La Bohème*, an opera about life and love among the writers and artists of 19th-century Paris. The first part of the opera takes place on Christmas Eve, so Marta and Plácido did enjoy a little of the traditional holiday spirit, even though Christmas is not celebrated in Israel.

If Domingo was feeling homesick in Tel Aviv, he had a great deal of company. The Hebrew National Opera drew performers from all over the world, and Domingo learned to perform with casts that resembled the makeup of the United Nations. In one production of *La traviata*, for example, Domingo sang in Italian; the baritone who played his father sang in Hungarian; the soprano who played Violetta sang in German; and the chorus sang in Hebrew. For a production of Mozart's *Don Giovanni*, based on the story of the legendary seducer Don Juan, the conductor was British, and the cast included two Mexicans, a Spaniard, a Japanese, an Italian, a Greek, and a black American. "Such casting," Domingo recalled, "was considered absolutely normal."

Years after his stint in Tel Aviv, Domingo said, "Israel gave me an awareness of worlds outside the one I was familiar with." He had lived only in Spain and Mexico, countries where nearly everyone was Catholic and spoke Spanish. But Israel had been settled by Jews from many countries, and Domingo soon grew accustomed to hearing a medley of languages wherever he went. His own grasp of languages improved, largely through watching movies with subtitles in French, English, and Hebrew. He learned the basics of those languages to add to his native Spanish and the smattering of Italian he had picked up. He was also excited by the musical sophistication of audiences in Israel. "There were always people from Poland, Russia, Rumania, Yugoslavia, Bulgaria, Germany, Czechoslovakia, Austria, Hungary, and elsewhere in the audience," he noted, "and all of them had a great appetite for music." So many people in Tel Aviv wanted to hear opera that the company could stage as many as 50 performances of a given opera during a season, and each would be well attended. The result was an atmosphere of interest and support that was very encouraging to a young singer.

The atmosphere may have been good, but the schedule was daunting. During his first 6 months in Tel Aviv, Domingo performed 43 times in 4 operas: *La Bohème*, *La traviata*, *Madama Butterfly*, and *Faust*. He knew the first three well, but he had little time to prepare for *Faust*, a French opera by Charles-François Gounod about an old man who sells his soul to the devil in exchange for youth and pleasure. The opening performance, in which Ornelas sang the lead soprano role, went well, but Domingo ran into

A view of a residential neighborhood in Tel Aviv, Israel. During his two and a half years at the Hebrew National Opera, Domingo was inspired by the mixture of nationalities and languages in cosmopolitan Tel Aviv and by the passion for music that united the city's residents.

serious trouble the second time. During an important aria, his voice cracked twice. He was embarrassed not only for himself but for Ornelas, who had to sing right after him.

To Domingo's astonishment, the reviews of the performance said nothing of his vocal problems. All the same, he offered to resign from the company. But the directors told him, "Plácido, here you have a chance to learn, and one mistake means nothing. We trust you, and we want you to continue." Looking back, he considered that vote of confidence "the biggest boost anyone has ever given me."

Shortly afterward, Domingo learned what may have been his single most important lesson about singing. Ornelas had previously told him that his voice was not carrying well when he sang high notes; Iglesias now convinced the opera company to give Domingo a few days off so that he could work on improving his voice. Domingo, Iglesias, and Ornelas went to the auditorium between rehearsals, and Domingo sang while the others tried to figure out what was wrong. It was Iglesias who discovered the problem. Years before, when Domingo was taking gym classes, he had been taught to breathe the way athletes do, with his chest expanded and his stomach in. Singers, on the other hand, are supposed to breathe by pushing out the abdomen and expanding the diaphragm, the muscular body just below the chest cavity. Because he had never had formal voice training, Domingo had not learned the proper method of breath control. Once he realized what the trouble was, he was able to correct it. The breathing and muscle-control exercises that Domingo worked on in Tel Aviv with Iglesias became the basis of his lifelong singing technique. In 1985, the British writer Daniel Snowman observed in his book *The World of Plácido Domingo* that Domingo had "the stomach muscles of a weightlifter."

After their six-month contract ran out, Domingo and Ornelas were asked to stay with the Hebrew National Opera for another year. They agreed and ended up staying a total of two and a half years before deciding that it was time to move on. By that time, Domingo had received offers to sing in several American productions and wanted to audition for as many opera companies as he could. He and Ornelas had also decided that they were ready to start a family, and they wanted their child to be born in Mexico. By the time he left Israel in 1965, Domingo had sung in 10 different operas for a total of 280 performances—an average of almost 1 performance every 3 days. Few tenors before or since have matched the stamina, energy, and dedication that he developed during his time in Israel.

Domingo's first stop after leaving Israel was Italy, where he auditioned for several opera companies. He and Ornelas then went on to Spain. It was his first visit to his homeland since he, Mari Pepa, and Aunt Agustina had left Madrid for Mexico years before, and he found that returning to the country of his birth stirred up his emotions. "As we landed in Madrid," he confessed, "I held Marta's hand and tried unsuccessfully to hold back my tears. . . . My feelings toward Spain had lain dormant in me for a long time, and that visit awakened them."

The Domingos at home in New York City. In 1966, when he realized that he would be singing regularly in New York, Domingo purchased a house in the area, and his wife and newborn son came from Mexico to join him.

After visiting with relatives, the Domingos flew to the United States, where Plácido had been engaged to sing Georges Bizet's *Carmen* in Washington, D.C. Domingo had the lead role of Don José, the soldier who falls in love with the Gypsy Carmen, deserts the army in order to live with her, and finally kills her in a jealous rage when she leaves him for a bullfighter. Domingo had sung *Carmen* many times in Tel Aviv, and he delivered a fine performance in Washington; as a result, he was invited to appear in *Carmen* at the New York City Opera.

Domingo's City Opera debut came four days earlier than expected. While he was rehearsing there for his appearance in *Carmen*, the tenor slated to sing in *Madama Butterfly* became ill, and Domingo was asked to replace him. This experience would be repeated when he made his Metropolitan Opera debut several years later.

Marta Domingo, who was pregnant, had stayed behind in Mexico City. On October 21, as Domingo was making his debut in *Carmen*, his son Plácido was born. The following day, Domingo was able to fly to Mexico to see the baby, whom everyone called Placi. But the very next day he was booked to sing in Puebla, Mexico, and then it was back to New York for more performances of *Carmen*, followed by his first appearance in Philadelphia. Then, on New Year's Day, 1966, he made his debut in his home country of Spain, singing in three operas from different regions of Mexico. The performances were staged in the Teatro del Liceo in Barcelona, the same theater where his mother had performed before her marriage.

A new phase in Domingo's life began with the New Year. The New York City Opera wanted him to appear in a number of productions, so he took up residence in the United States, bringing Marta and Placi to join him. The Domingo family settled into a home in Teaneck, New Jersey, not far from New York City. For several years Domingo divided his time between the City Opera and various other companies in the United States, Mexico, and Europe. Each year brought new experiences—first performances in particular operas, opera houses, or cities.

One "first" was especially important to Domingo because of his pride in his Spanish heritage—the leading role in the City Opera's 1966 production of a work that had never before been performed in North America, *Don Rodrigo*, by Argentine composer Alberto Ginastera. The unveiling of a new opera is in itself something special: Few contemporary composers write operas, and few modern operas have won favor with audiences. Most of the operas that are performed around the world each year are established favorites from the 18th, 19th, and very early 20th centuries; the operas of Puccini and Verdi alone account for nearly half of all performances. Domingo was thrilled to introduce a new work to the public, even though the long, intense rehearsals were grueling, and the music—less melodic than the traditional favorites—was difficult to sing. "But for the public," he remarked, "it was an exciting evening: they had not seen a contemporary opera of that stature in a long time. For a young Spaniard to be able to sing, on such an occasion, the role of a Spanish king, and in Spanish, was an unforgettable experience. There was much praise for the work, for the production, and, fortunately, for my singing. I did not fully realize at that moment what it all meant for my future. There I was, just a month after my twenty-fifth birthday and just eight months after leaving Tel Aviv, enjoying great success in New York. It hardly seemed possible."

The following year Domingo made his first appearances in South America, singing in Lima, Peru, and Santiago, Chile. He was rapturously received by the Spanish-speaking audiences there; in Lima the singers who made up the chorus were so enthusiastic that they accompanied Domingo to the airport and gave him a farewell serenade.

Like all opera singers, Domingo knew that some opera houses are more prestigious than others. He could not feel that he had truly arrived until he had sung in what he liked to call the Big Four—the four opera houses that are associated with the highest standards, the most important new productions, and the best singers. They are the Staatsoper, or State Opera, in Vienna, Austria; the Metropolitan Opera in New York City; La Scala in Milan, Italy; and the Royal Opera at Covent Garden in London.

Domingo's first Big Four debut was in Vienna in 1967. It was also the first time he sang the leading role in Verdi's *Don Carlos*, another opera based on Spanish history—the story of the tragic and tangled loves of King Philip II of Spain, his son Prince Carlos, and Carlos's stepmother. Domingo's Staatsoper debut very nearly ended in disaster. The rehearsal had taken place in a rehearsal room, and Domingo had never actually been on the stage until the performance started. No one had warned him that the Staatsoper stage is steeply raked—that is, it slopes very drastically from back to front. Domingo, filled with excitement and nervous energy, waited backstage for his cue and then "came charging out like a young bull," as he described it. Caught off guard by the steep angle of the stage, he almost launched himself right into the audience. He managed to put the brakes on, however, and the performance was a great success.

Having proved himself before the demanding Viennese audience, Domingo was ready to tackle the other major opera houses. The second of his Big Four conquests was the Metropolitan Opera in New York, where he appeared in 1968. Like his debut at the New York City Opera, the event came about somewhat unexpectedly.

When the Met signed him, Domingo was still singing frequently at the City Opera. Because the City Opera and the Met are right next to one another in the Lincoln Center complex, Domingo was able to shuttle from one house to the other as he prepared for his October 2 debut at the Met. The Met management had scheduled him to take over the leading male role in Francesco Cilea's *Adriana Lecouvreur*, an opera based on the life and loves of an 18th-century Parisian actress. Franco Corelli, one of the top tenors of the generation before Domingo's, was starring in the initial performances, and Domingo was to replace him for the latter part of the season.

The new Metropolitan Opera House in New York City, photographed after its opening in 1966. Domingo made his debut at the Met two years later, while he was under contract for a full schedule at the neighboring New York City Opera.

In the week leading up to his Met debut, Domingo appeared in two productions at the City Opera. On Saturday, September 28, he was called to the Met to take the tenor part at an extra afternoon rehearsal of *Turandot*. He completed the rehearsal and drove back to Teaneck to have dinner with his family. At that time Marta Domingo was pregnant with the couple's second child, and Plácido's parents had come from Mexico City both to be with Marta and to attend their son's big debut at the Met. The family ate an early dinner that Saturday, because Domingo planned to go back to the Met in the evening to hear Corelli sing his last performance of *Adriana Lecouvreur*. After dinner, while Domingo was shaving, the telephone rang. It was Rudolf Bing, the manager of the Met.

"How do you feel?" Bing asked.

"Very well, thank you," Domingo replied, completely mystified by the call.

"That's wonderful," said Bing, "because you are going to make your Metropolitan debut tonight." Corelli, it turned out, felt unwell and had decided not to perform. Domingo's debut would take place five days ahead of schedule. Fortunately, he had already learned the part.

Domingo got dressed in a hurry and set out for the Met with his father for company. As he drove down the West Side Highway, he began to warm up his voice. At one point he was held up in traffic and noticed that the people in the next car were looking at him and laughing. By this time he had opened up to full volume, with all the facial distortion that such singing requires, and he realized that he probably looked quite comical. He rolled down his window and asked the onlookers, "Where are you going?"

"To the Met," they answered.

"Well, don't laugh, because you'll be hearing me in a few minutes!" he told them as his car pulled away.

That night's performance began 20 minutes late. An announcement was made to the audience that "a young singer" would replace the ailing Corelli. The young singer was understandably

Franco Corelli, one of the leading tenors of the 1950s and 1960s. Domingo was scheduled to take over Corelli's role in Adriana Lecouvreur *on October 2, 1968; he was unexpectedly pressed into service five days early when Corelli suddenly declared himself unable to perform.*

nervous. He was also angry at having been called to substitute with only half an hour's notice—usually a substitute singer has most of a day in which to prepare. But, he recalled, "The evening was a wonderful one for me. . . . Everyone was helping me to do my best, to accomplish something I had been dreaming about for years." The evening produced a bonus for Domingo, too: By the time his official debut came around four days later, he was calm and relaxed, and his singing received excellent reviews from the opera critics.

The Domingos' second son was born two weeks after the Met debut. They named the boy Alvaro, but they gave him the middle name Maurizio, which was the name of Domingo's character in *Adriana Lecouvreur.* On the night Alvaro was born, Domingo sang in the City Opera production of Ruggiero Leoncavallo's *Pagliacci* (The Clowns), an opera about love and jealousy among a troupe of circus performers. In one scene, Domingo's character is supposed to throw pieces of candy to the chorus, but on that night he threw cigars with IT'S A BOY printed on the wrappers.

A few weeks later, Domingo appeared in his first radio broadcast from the Met. Live broadcasts of the Saturday afternoon performances are a tradition at the Met, and taking part in them is considered an honor. Domingo had not expected to appear in one for some time, but Corelli was again unable to perform, and the backup tenor also became ill shortly before airtime. Once more Domingo was pressed into service, this time to sing the part of Cavaradossi in *Tosca*—fortunately, one that he knew by heart. He had only a few minutes to prepare, and he remembered Rudolf Bing watching him anxiously from the wings, perhaps fearing that he would try to run away. But the broadcast went smoothly, and Domingo later appeared in other broadcast performances.

Having proved himself at the Met, Domingo was ready to make his Italian debut in the northern city of Verona, in July 1969. Italy was the birthplace of opera, and even though many countries have produced outstanding composers, conductors, and singers, Italy has always claimed the lion's share of the world's great opera composers and performers. Italians are especially proud of their tradition of producing legendary tenors, such as Enrico Caruso, Beniamino Gigli, Giovanni Martinelli, Tito Schipa, and (more recently) Luciano Pavarotti. As he prepared for his debut, Domingo became aware that people all over Verona were asking, "Who is this tenor, this Spaniard? Does he have a voice?" To add to the pressure, he was taking on a new role, Calaf in Puccini's *Turandot*, which required him to sing one of the most famous and difficult of all tenor arias, "Nessun dorma."

The Verona *Turandot* was a remarkable experience for Domingo. It was staged in an ancient Roman amphitheater, and the

The famed Teatro alla Scala in Milan, Italy, photographed in 1964. Milan's operagoers are notoriously hard to please, but they gave Domingo a warm reception when he made his La Scala debut in 1969, singing the title role in Giuseppe Verdi's Ernani.

role of Turandot was sung by the great Swedish soprano Birgit Nilsson, who so dazzled Domingo with her vocal power and artistry that he almost forgot to sing. While the opera was taking place, American astronauts were making the first landing on the moon. *Turandot* is the opera that contains the chorus to the moon that had so deeply moved Domingo when he first heard it years before in Mexico. Now hearing it again in Verona as the moon rose over the amphitheater, he was deeply moved once more. "I well remember the feeling of amazement, as the moon shone over us in that nineteen-hundred-year-old Roman ruin, that people were walking up there at that moment," he wrote.

Verona gave Domingo its wholehearted approval, but he still had to conquer La Scala, Italy's most prestigious opera house and the third of his Big Four debuts. That event took place in December 1969.

Built in 1778, Milan's Teatro alla Scala, as it is officially known, has been the scene of many memorable performances. Throughout the years, the leading Italian composers all wrote operas especially to be staged there, and Arturo Toscanini, one of the greatest conductors of all time, served as music director there between 1898 and 1929. "When you stand on the stage of La Scala and look into that beautiful auditorium," Domingo later said, "you cannot help thinking that nearly every celebrated singer from Mozart's day to our own has performed there."

La Scala is the pinnacle that every opera singer wants to ascend, but the climb is a dangerous one. Milan's operagoers are notorious for their scorn of anyone who fails to meet their lofty standards, and even a great singer having an off night is likely to endure boos, hisses, and rude remarks. Fortunately, Domingo was in top form, singing the title role in Verdi's *Ernani*—the story of a Spanish prince turned outlaw—and the Milanese gave him a hearty ovation. He especially enjoyed his time in Milan because it was the holiday season. His parents flew in from Mexico, and the entire family was able to celebrate Noche Buena, Christmas, and Three Kings Day.

Domingo rehearses a scene with soprano Renata Scotto and baritone Sherrill Milnes. Always a tireless worker, Domingo sang more than 700 performances during the first 10 years of his career.

Only one of the Big Four opera houses remained—Covent Garden. Domingo made his debut there in *Tosca* in December 1971. Unfortunately, the event took place under tragic conditions. Marie Collier, the soprano who was to sing the leading role opposite Domingo, died the night before the production opened. A substitute was found, and the show went on, but Domingo's satisfaction at having finally performed in all of the world's leading opera houses was muted by his sadness over Collier's death.

By 1971, a decade after his debut in Monterrey, Domingo had succeeded in carving out a place for himself in the world of opera. The records he had meticulously kept in little green leatherbound notebooks since the start of his career showed that he had sung in more than 700 performances. He had mastered several dozen roles. He had sung in scores of opera houses, including the Big Four. These were remarkable achievements, but they were only the first stage of a major operatic career. Now Domingo had to prove that he could sustain his level of achievement over a long period of steady performing.

Domingo made his debut as a conductor in 1973. He has long been admired by his colleagues for being not only a singer but an all-around musician, a talent that he attributes to his early training on the piano.

CHAPTER SIX

A Singer's Life

As he moved through the 1970s and into the 1980s, Plácido Domingo continued to pursue his goal of becoming one of the world's great opera singers. By 1983, music critic Bernard Holland could accurately say of Domingo in a *New York Times Magazine* article: "His career has been marked by an insatiable appetite, almost a gluttony, for more roles, more performances, more places to sing." While pursuing a rigorous schedule of live performances, Domingo also began to develop other facets of his musicianship, such as making recordings. He knew that opera singers are often judged as much by their recordings as by their live performances. He also knew that record sales not only boost a singer's income but also help create future audiences: Someone who buys a record and enjoys it may make an effort to attend a performance. The reverse is also true: Those who enjoy live opera also tend to buy records.

There is often great competition among record companies to sign up promising new singers, and each opera star, as he or she becomes successful, strives to make recordings of all the best-known and most popular operas. Sometimes a singer will record a given opera more than once; Domingo, for example, has made three recordings of Verdi's *Aïda*. He recorded his first *Aïda* in 1970, early in his career, when his voice was fresh and youthful, although not yet fully disciplined. The second recording came in 1981, during Domingo's period of greatest activity, when his voice still had considerable freshness but had also been polished and refined by years of experience. He made the third recording in 1991, by which time his voice had lost some of its youthful vibrancy but had gained much depth and richness.

The three recordings present a good example of how a singer's voice changes with time and use. Good young tenor voices have a sound that is sometimes described as "bright" or "brilliant"—a clear, penetrating quality. More mature tenor voices have less of this edge, or brilliance, and are generally smoother, more mellow, and a bit deeper. But a tenor who overuses his voice—who sings too much too fast or who tackles difficult roles too early in his career—may damage his voice, making it rougher, harsher, and less flexible.

Domingo and soprano Aprile Millo sing a duet in Verdi's Aïda, *one of the great favorites in the operatic repertoire. Between 1970 and 1991, Domingo recorded the opera three times, refining his approach as his voice grew deeper and richer with age.*

Throughout the early part of his career, Domingo was frequently warned by music critics that he was singing too much and was risking the health of his voice. Yet he proved them wrong: Although he did sing much more often than most tenors, he tolerated it very well, and eventually the critics had to acknowledge that he had known what he was doing.

Domingo also proved that he was able to sing a wider variety of roles—and at an earlier age—than many tenors. By 1982 he had sung 82 different roles in performance or on recordings. After suffering his only bout of voice trouble after a 1968 performance of *Lohengrin*, he steered clear of Wagner's demanding operas until 1984. But as early as 1975 he decided he was ready to take on another very taxing dramatic opera, Verdi's *Otello*, which is based on Shakespeare's *Othello*, a tragic drama concerning jealousy and betrayal. Most tenors do not approach this difficult role until fairly late in their career because the demands it makes have contributed to the ruin of many young singers' voices. "In itself, the second act of *Otello* is as exhausting for the tenor as most entire operas," Domingo once asserted, "and there are three other acts to be dealt with as well." *Otello* is generally avoided by tenors until they approach the age of 50.

Domingo appears in Verdi's Otello, *which the singer first tackled at the age of 34. He was warned that the demanding role could ruin his voice, but he handled it with ease; he went on to perform in many more productions of* Otello *and starred in a film version of the opera.*

Domingo admitted that in agreeing to sing *Otello* at the age of 34, he was "pitting my own instincts about my vocal health and capabilities against the admonitions of the experts." One such expert was Rolf Liebermann, an official of Germany's Hamburg Opera. Domingo gave a performance in *La Bohème* in Hamburg in September 1975, just before he was scheduled to sing *Otello* for the first time. On the night of the performance, Liebermann said, "Keep your ears open as you listen to Plácido, because this will probably be his last *Bohème*." Like many others, Liebermann believed that *Otello* would destroy Domingo's voice—or at least roughen it so badly that he could no longer sing in lighter, more lyric operas such as *La Bohème*.

The first performance of *Otello* ranks in Domingo's estimation as "one of the most important dates in my career." The entire opera world was waiting to see whether he would succeed or self-destruct. He had risked his voice, but his instincts had been sound. "Everything went splendidly, and the public and press reacted with great enthusiasm," he recalled. To allay fears that he had lost his ability to sing lighter opera, he sandwiched a performance of *Tosca* between two of his five appearances in the production of *Otello*.

A few months later, Liebermann called Domingo and invited him to appear in *La Bohème*. As he recalled in his autobiography, Domingo could not resist gloating a bit. "How is this possible?" he asked. "You said no more *Bohème*s for Plácido." Liebermann sheepishly replied that he had been concerned only about Domingo's well-being. Subsequently, *Otello* became one of Domingo's most celebrated roles; he not only recorded it but also starred in a movie version of the opera, released in 1986.

Domingo's recording career began in 1968. His first recordings were selections of well-known arias; in 1969, he made his first recording of a complete opera, Verdi's *Il trovatore* (The Troubador). His recording career then took off as Domingo threw himself into this new activity with his usual energy. In 1971, for example, he found himself engaged in seven different recording projects while maintaining his heavy schedule of live performances. The pace continued: In 1977, 11 new recordings by Domingo of complete operas appeared in 11 successive months. By 1982, he had made more than 70 recordings. By 1991, the total approached 200.

When he first started recording, Domingo acquired a reputation as a singer who was willing to spend hour after hour in the studio, doing repeated takes—that is, singing the same music over and over in an attempt to get every note just right. Baritone Sherrill Milnes worked with Domingo during the 1969 recording of *Il trovatore*, in which the tenor sings "Di quella pira" ("That funeral pyre"), one of opera's most demanding arias: It has to be sung at full volume and at high speed, and it ends with not one but two high C's, notes that were sometimes hard for Domingo to hit. During the recording session, Domingo had trouble with those high C's. "He stood there with a towel around his neck in front of the full male chorus—forty guys, each of them probably thinking they could do better," Milnes remembered. "You just had to love him for it, standing full of courage in front of the world, so to speak, soaking wet and with that stunning voice cracking until finally he got it right."

Domingo hard at work in the recording studio. With almost 200 recordings to his credit between 1968 and 1991, Domingo has been noted for both the variety of music he records and his relentless drive for perfection.

Most of Domingo's recordings have been of operatic music, either complete operas or collections of arias. In 1972 he made an album of arias that had been favored by the great Caruso, and in 1975 he recorded *The Operatic Duo of the Century*, an album of "opera's greatest hits," with diva Leontyne Price. Yet he has also recorded a wide variety of other kinds of music, including pop tunes. In 1981 he collaborated with pop star John Denver on an album of ballads called *Perhaps Love*, which was more successful than even its producers expected, selling more than 1 million copies. That same year he made an album of Christmas songs. This type of crossover recording, as it is called in the music industry, allowed Domingo to reach a much wider audience than he could reach by singing opera alone. He was criticized for it by some opera lovers, who felt that Domingo should save his voice for "serious" singing.

Domingo shares the spotlight with pop country singer John Denver at a 1984 gala celebrating the 100th year of the Metropolitan Opera. Three years earlier, Domingo and Denver had collaborated on Perhaps Love, *and album of romantic ballads that sold more than 1 million copies.*

Although the purists tend to emphasize the elite or exclusive quality of opera, there is a long tradition of opera singers crossing over into popular music. Adelina Patti, the world's reigning soprano throughout the second half of the 19th century, used to delight audiences by having a piano pushed onstage after an opera performance and singing "Home, Sweet Home," "Comin' Thro' the Rye," and other popular favorites. Caruso, who was born in Naples, Italy, frequently sang "O sole mio" and other popular Neapolitan melodies. The great operatic baritone Ezio Pinza appeared in the Rodgers and Hammerstein musical *South Pacific*. Indeed, until almost the middle of the 20th century, opera was itself a form of popular music, and the leading opera singers were as well known to the general public as Madonna and Michael Jackson are today.

For these reasons, Domingo has always rejected the idea that opera singers should not sing music that appeals to a wide audience. He also believes that people who hear and enjoy his popular recordings might become interested in opera. As evidence, he can quote letters from people who told him that the *Perhaps Love* album had awakened their curiosity about opera, prompting them to attend their first opera performance and in some cases turning them into opera lovers.

There was a financial reason as well for Domingo's ventures into popular music. Admittedly, his income from performances was substantial: By the early 1980s, he was earning $8,000 for each performance at the Metropolitan Opera (this was the top fee then paid by the Met) and more than $20,000 a night in some European opera houses. But recordings, which may continue to bring in money over many years, are regarded by singers as a form of long-term security for themselves and their families. "I don't have much of a head for business," Domingo remarked, "but when I record an obscure opera like Weber's *Oberon*, a terribly demanding and difficult opera for the tenor, I can see how little it sells around the world. *Oberon* is definitely not going to provide an income for my children, but *Perhaps Love* will."

Ezio Pinza sings a duet with Mary Martin in a 1949 performance of the Rodgers and Hammerstein musical South Pacific. *By branching out into popular music, Domingo was merely following the example of earlier opera stars such as Pinza and Adelina Patti.*

Apart from the financial rewards involved, Domingo truly enjoys singing many types of music. One facet of his recording career that he finds particularly rewarding is Hispanic music. He feels strongly about the need to preserve and promote the Hispanic musical heritage, ranging from folk and pop tunes to opera and other serious works by Spanish-speaking composers. He feels a special responsibility toward the Hispanic community in the United States, where he spends about a third of his time. "It is my impression," he once asserted, "that this group's cultural roots are being ignored or forgotten in a shameful way."

Because of his parents' theatrical careers, Domingo grew up surrounded not just by zarzuela music but also by Hispanic dance music and the ballads of Spanish, Mexican, and Latin American composers and singers. At the beginning of his professional career, when he intended to specialize in zarzuela, he also considered doing Spanish-language musical comedy or going into film work like the popular Mexican singers Jorge Negrete and Pedro Infante did. "By then, however, my romance with opera was beginning," he said, "and there was no going back."

Recalling those early enthusiasms, Domingo has made many recordings of zarzuela music and Spanish-language songs. In 1974 he recorded *Music of My Country*, an album of zarzuela arias. His 1981 album *Tangos*, a collection of Argentine dance songs, became the best-selling record in the history of the recording company Deutsche Grammophon. *Adoro* (1982) consisted of popular Mexican songs, and *Always in My Heart* (1983) was a selection from the works of Cuban composer Ernesto Lecuona. *Romanzas and Zarzuelas* (1986) was another collection of zarzuela music, which Domingo has also performed in many concerts worldwide. "Apart from zarzuela, which is an art form that originated in Spain itself," he says, "I am trying to interest Hispanic Americans living in the States in the music of their own countries of origin—and there are some glorious treasures to be found."

Domingo has taken special pleasure in performing in Spain. One extraordinary experience was an outdoor concert he gave in Madrid in 1982. There were seats for 20,000 people; the authorities expected that perhaps as many as 30,000 others would occupy the standing room. To Domingo's delighted amazement more than 250,000 showed up, almost everyone standing for 2 hours to hear him sing. Over the years, he has given many performances in Spain, especially in the Teatro del Liceo in Barcelona, and he spoke often of a desire to support and stimulate the Spanish population's interest in opera. He encouraged the building of Seville's new opera house, called the Maestranza, which opened in 1991. Domingo sang at the opening of the Maestranza and agreed to serve as one of its musical advisers.

Conducting is another aspect of musicianship to which Domingo devoted growing attention as his career progressed. As a young man, he had sat in on some conducting classes at the National Conservatory in Mexico City and later had conducted some performances of his parents' zarzuela company. He had become fascinated by the role of the conductor—the individual who animates and controls the entire performance.

"I always liked the idea of conducting, even before I sang," he told an interviewer in 1972. He let opera managers know that he was interested in building a secondary career as a conductor, and in 1973 he made his conducting debut, at the New York City Opera. The opera he conducted was *La traviata*, the same one in which he had made his debut as a lead singer more than a decade earlier. He went on to conduct performances in a number of opera houses, including the Vienna Staatsoper and Covent Garden. His conducting debut at the Metropolitan Opera took place in 1984, with *La Bohème*.

Domingo's only problem as a conductor was that he sometimes began to sing along with the tenors as he stood on the podium. He gradually learned to resist this impulse, however, and earned the respect of some of the world's leading conductors, such as James Levine and Zubin Mehta, for his conducting ability and his thorough knowledge of music.

"Conducting a whole work," Domingo has stated, "is a more fulfilling experience than singing or playing parts of it." He has declared that when he is no longer able to sing, he will launch another career as a conductor.

Perhaps the single most impressive aspect of Domingo's career during the 1970s and 1980s was the grueling schedule he maintained. In a single three-week period in early 1982, for example, he sang in two performances of Vincenzo Bellini's *Norma*, two performances of *La Bohème*, a performance of Verdi's *Requiem*, and a concert with soprano Tatiana Troyanos, all at the Met; he also sang in a peace concert at St. Patrick's Cathedral, teamed up with Miss Piggy of the Muppets for a concert at Radio City Music Hall, and rehearsed for the Met's new production of Jacques Offenbach's *Les Contes d'Hoffmann* (The Tales of Hoffmann).

Domingo's schedule made him a very frequent flyer. In the fall of 1981 he gave multiple performances of seven different operas in locations as diverse as New York; Monterrey, Mexico; Munich and Cologne, Germany; London; Monte Carlo, Monaco; and San

By the 1980s, Domingo had become an international star of the first magnitude. In this photo, fans unable to get tickets for a sold-out performance at London's Covent Garden watch Domingo on a giant TV screen set up outside the opera house.

Francisco. Sandwiched between these performances were an appearance at a recording-industry convention in Puerto Rico, interviews with all the mass media in the cities where he performed, the study of new roles, and recording sessions for several albums that were released in 1982.

Domingo was able to sing so many different operas in such a short time because, unlike most opera singers, he did not need a coach to help him learn new roles. Traditionally, singers rely upon a coach to play the piano score of a new opera while they learn the words; there have even been singers who did not know how to read music and had to be guided in the memorization of every note. But Domingo's early musical training—especially his training on the piano—gave him an enormous advantage. It allowed him to teach himself new roles at home or in hotel rooms and rehearsal halls scattered around the world. Typically, he plays through the piano score of a new opera, accompanying himself while he learns each note and phrase, studying words and music simultaneously. Although he has occasionally sought help from coaches in both singing and in such matters as proper pronunciation of a foreign language, he has generally taught and coached himself. Throughout his career, he has also received much assistance from his wife.

Although Marta Domingo and her husband sang as partners during their Tel Aviv days, she decided to give up her career when their sons were born. Her musical knowledge and expertise, however, helped her serve as a coach—and, when necesary, a critic—to her husband. He dedicated his autobiography to her, calling her "the inspiration and on many occasions the guide in my career."

Success never comes without a price, and in Domingo's case part of the penalty was a somewhat fragmented family life. Although he was a devoted father, he was often away from his sons while they were growing up. "It's awful when you realize that you see more of people in cities where you sing than of your own children," he once said, and he never forgot that his children and his wife were making many sacrifices for his career.

Plácido and Marta Domingo enjoy an evening out in New York in 1983. Domingo's only regret about stardom was the amount of time he was forced to spend away from his family while his two sons, Placi and Alvaro, were growing up.

The family remained in Teaneck, New Jersey, for a few years after Domingo's career took off. After a while, however, the Domingos decided that they wanted their sons to be raised as Europeans, and for nine years they made their principal home in Barcelona. José, Domingo's son by his first marriage, settled in London, where the Domingos purchased a house; they also owned a condominium in Monte Carlo, overlooking the Riviera beaches of the Mediterranean, and an apartment in New York City. Placi and Alvaro were enrolled in boarding school in Switzerland, and their parents shuttled from one residence to another according to Domingo's performance schedule. "We live out of a suitcase," Domingo remarked in 1982, when he was as busy as he had ever been.

His career made it impossible for him to spend long, unbroken stretches of time with his family, but Domingo made a special effort to be with them for vacations, holidays, and celebrations of special occasions. In 1980, when his parents celebrated their 40th wedding anniversary, he invited them to join him for mass at a church in Mexico City. When they arrived at the church, they found the entire Domingo clan and many of their friends from the theater there, along with a symphony orchestra that played while their son serenaded them.

Occasionally, Domingo was able to combine work and family togetherness. In the summer of 1983, he was booked for several months' work on a movie version of *Carmen*, to be shot on location in Spain, where the opera is set. It was the longest stretch of time Domingo had spent in Spain since he was seven years old.

The setting for the film was the ancient white-walled town of Ronda, which is perched high on a steep cliff above the Guadalevin River in southern Spain. A vivid description of Ronda and an account of the filming of *Carmen* can be found in Daniel Snowman's *World of Plácido Domingo*. Snowman describes the chaotic but comfortable atmosphere of the house Domingo rented for the season, where he, Marta, a secretary, a cook, the two boys, and six or eight relatives and friends might be found singing by the

Domingo in the role of Don José in Bizet's Carmen. *While starring in the film version of the opera, made in southern Spain in 1983, Domingo reacquainted himself with his native country, which he had left at the age of seven.*

piano or lounging by the pool in the courtyard. For six days each week, however, Domingo was fully absorbed in the film project, which included scenes shot on the mountainside above Ronda and in the town's bullring.

At one point during the filming, Domingo had to sneak away. He had promised a group of young musicians in the town that he would be a judge at their Festival of Song. Unexpectedly, director Francesco Rosi decided to keep shooting during the evening in order to complete the scene in which Don José, the renegade army officer, arrives on horseback at the mountain hideout of the Gypsy smugglers. For some of the more dangerous riding scenes, a double was used, and Domingo seized the opportunity to jump into a taxi and speed off to Ronda, where the young people were waiting in a local movie theater. Snowman's account of the episode is highly revealing:

The place erupts with a roar such as only a thousand exuberant teenagers can make and Plácido in his dusty Don
José outfit, sweat beading his brow and filtering through his
artificial chin stubble, marches out onto the stage. . . . He
goes over to the MC's microphone, hands raised, and gets
instant silence. . . . He shouldn't really be here, he explains
with a guilty grin, but is supposed to be filming out in the
mountains. But to tell the truth he is very happy to have
been able to make it. Massive applause. He can't stay as long
as he had originally hoped (groans and long faces) . . . but
(yes?) . . . perhaps people wouldn't mind if instead of judg-
ing the competition as he had intended he might just sing a
song himself. . . . This is a completely unexpected bonus
and a thousand throats shout themselves silly with excitement. . . . He slouches over the rickety upright piano in the
corner looking like a character in a John Ford Western, sits
himself down on the stool, and bangs out the accompaniment to "Jurame." . . . The applause after "Jurame" cracks
out like gunfire. Plácido gets up, his spurs get tangled in the
electric wiring, and he trips his way back to the microphone
and addresses the audience again. He signals to the wings
for another drink of *agua* [water] and knocks it back like
any bar pianist. OK, an encore (roars of approval), but I
really shouldn't. Then back to his corner for a tremendous
rendition of "Granada." . . . There is almost a stampede.
The youngsters are ecstatic and feel that they have received
double bounty, two songs from their hero when they had expected none. The whole thing has taken less than fifteen
minutes and immediately . . . Plácido is speeding, courtesy
of the waiting Antonio, back out of town and towards the
darkened sierras. As he clambers back up to the film location exactly one hour after slipping off, he chuckles to himself.

The episode sums up many of the essential qualities of Domingo's
career—hard work, a frantic pace, and constant motion, combined
with a genuine love of performing and a great generosity of spirit.

Domingo and Jessye Norman in a 1991 performance of Wagner's Parsifal
*at the Metropolitan Opera. By meeting the vocal challenges of Wagner's
music, Domingo entered the 1990s with a whole new repertoire at his
command.*

CHAPTER SEVEN

Thirty Years

It is part of the tradition of opera that singers who rise to greatness at the same time must become rivals. Stories of feuds or rivalries between sopranos or tenors have been part of opera lore for decades. One of the best-known recent examples is the feud between Maria Callas and Renata Tebaldi in the 1950s. Their rivalry divided the world's opera lovers into two camps: One was either a follower of Callas or a supporter of Tebaldi. Each singer pretended to deny that there was any competition, however. "How could we be rivals?" Callas said to a reporter from *Time* magazine. "I am champagne, and she is Coca-Cola."

In the late 1970s and early 1980s, a similar rivalry appeared to dominate the opera world as two tenors vied for supremacy. One was Plácido Domingo. The other was a rotund, exuberant Italian named Luciano Pavarotti. Five years older than Domingo, Pavarotti began his rise through the opera ranks a few years earlier, although his debut at the Metropolitan Opera did not come until a month or so after Domingo's. Gifted with a high, pure, ringing tenor,

Pavarotti made his mark in lyric operas, such as Donizetti's *La Fille du régiment* (Daughter of the Regiment) and *L'elisir d'amore* (The Love Potion), that call for nimble singing in the high register and contain many chances for a tenor to hit showstopping high C's. Pavarotti excelled in such works; one of his first albums, in fact, was called *King of the High C's.*

Early in his career, Pavarotti also demonstrated a personal flair that won him admirers around the world, even among people who had no interest in opera. He appeared on television talk shows and gave numerous magazine interviews; he wrapped his considerable bulk in a mink coat for an advertisement; and he sang popular music as well as operatic music, both in concert and on recordings. Soon his face and voice—and the large white handkerchief with which he mopped his brow during concert performances—were familiar to millions of people, whereas Domingo was not so well known outside the operagoing community.

An incident in 1980 spurred Domingo to enter the popularity competition. Domingo arrived in London for an important new production at Covent Garden, only to find that the city's newspapers and magazines were filled with articles about Pavarotti, touting him as "the world's greatest tenor." Uncharacteristically, Domingo lost his temper. He realized that Pavarotti had built a very effective public relations machine, and he decided to do the same. He hired a new publicity manager and worked on strengthening his ties with the recording companies, which in turn increased their commitment to furthering his career.

By 1983 or 1984, Domingo had caught up to Pavarotti in the celebrity sweepstakes. Pavarotti plugged mink coats; Domingo appeared in ads for luxury wristwatches. Pavarotti sang with Frank Sinatra; Domingo sang with Miss Piggy. Pavarotti made a Hollywood movie (*Yes, Giorgio!*, which flopped with both audiences and critics); Domingo made his pop album with John Denver. Pavarotti was the subject of a cover story in *Time* magazine; Domingo made the cover of *Newsweek.*

A caricature of Luciano Pavarotti by artist Al Hirschfeld. For many years, Domingo and Pavarotti vied for the title of the world's leading tenor; although Domingo was sometimes annoyed by the attention lavished on Pavarotti, he always praised his rival's artistry.

How real was the rivalry? It is impossible to say. For the most part, the two men avoided attacking or criticizing one another directly. In his autobiography Domingo simply referred to Pavarotti as "one of the most celebrated tenors of our time" and described his voice as "incredibly beautiful." He added: "As to the much-discussed Pavarotti-Domingo 'rivalry,' it exists more vividly in the minds of certain journalists and fans than in those of the protagonists."

"I think audiences adore feuds," observed Jane Nemeth of the Philadelphia Opera Company in 1982. "They tend to like the 'opera' revolving around the opera. But I personally don't see how anyone can compare these two tenors."

In truth, the two men's voices and singing styles were very different, and their careers ran on parallel tracks only during the late 1970s and early to mid-1980s. Pavarotti established himself as the master of those operas—Puccini's in particular—that are suited to his lyric tenor voice, and Domingo made a name for himself as the master of a much broader repertoire—more than 80 roles as compared with Pavarotti's 35 or so—with special distinction in roles such as *Otello* and *Carmen* that suited his darker, deeper tenor.

By the late 1980s, the so-called battle of the tenors had largely faded from public view. Indeed, in 1990 the public was treated to an unprecedented treat—a concert featuring both Domingo and Pavarotti as well as José Carreras, a Spanish tenor who during the 1980s had come to be regarded as the closest rival of the other two.

The Three Tenors concert, as the event was soon known, took place in Rome on July 7. The setting was the Baths of Caracalla, the ruins of an immense complex of pools and bathhouses built by the Roman emperor Caracalla in the 3rd century A.D. The ancient stone walls and the leafy plane trees in the background gleamed under a full moon and a battery of stage lights. The orchestra warmed up under the direction of Zubin Mehta, and then the three tenors delivered a program that included opera arias and popular songs in a variety of languages. It was an evening of thrilling singing—and also of charming moments, as when the singers exchanged hugs and high-fives while making their exits and entrances. At the end of the concert they joined in a medley that included songs in French, German, and Italian as well as selections in English from the musicals *West Side Story* and *Cats*. Although only 6,000 people were able to attend the concert live, millions have seen it on television or videotape and heard the recorded version. In August 1991 the Three Tenors video rose to third place on the *Billboard* magazine best-seller list—"an unheard-of position for classical titles," in the words of the *New York Times*.

Domingo's life and career progressed without a hitch until September 1985, when a massive earthquake struck Mexico City, toppling buildings and wiping out entire neighborhoods. Domingo had an engagement in Chicago at the time, but as soon as he got word of the tragedy, he left at once for Mexico. News broadcasts showed him covered with grime, sifting through the rubble of fallen buildings alongside others who were searching for their friends and relatives. When all the debris was cleared away, the death toll stood at 7,000—including an aunt, an uncle, and two cousins of Domingo's. In the aftermath of the tragedy, Domingo canceled most of his scheduled performances for the 1985–86 season and instead organized a series of concerts and appearances that raised more than $1.5 million for aid to the earthquake victims. Domingo's parents had survived the earthquake, but in 1987, Plácido Domingo, Sr., died of natural causes, adding another sad note to a difficult time.

Despite family tragedies, the mid- and late 1980s found Domingo at the peak of his singing form: His 1984 *Lohengrin* at the Met

When a massive earth-
quake rocked Mexico City
in 1985, Domingo rushed
to the scene and worked
alongside the rescue crews.
During the following year,
he organized a number of
benefits to raise money for
the victims.

and his 1986 film version of *Otello* were especially praised by the critics. Domingo also appeared in a Public Broadcasting System TV production called "Domingo Salutes Seville," in which he sang excerpts from operas set in the city, and joined pop singers Gloria Estefan and Linda Ronstadt for a free concert of operatic and Hispanic music in New York's Central Park.

Back in 1977, when he was 36 years old, Domingo had justified his tremendous work load in an interview with the music writer Peter G. Davis: "I am in the prime time of life for a singer, and my voice seems to thrive on this kind of pacing. People have always told me, 'Plácido, slow down, save something for later.' But I feel I must take advantage of the best years of my career. I hope I will sing for 30 years, but I can't think 'save now and give more later'—how can I be sure I'll have the voice later? I want to sing now while it's all there."

By the late 1980s, Domingo's staying power provoked as much admiration as his singing. In 1989, for example, following a concert by Domingo in Seattle, Washington, the *Portland Oregonian* said, "During his years on the world operatic stage, Domingo . . . has maintained an impossibly busy schedule. . . . Listeners scrutinize him these days for signs of wear and tear, but on Friday night, at the Seattle Opera House, there was hardly a gray hair or a frayed vocal cord in evidence. . . . He continues to sing with as much vigor and forcefulness as he did when he started at the Metropolitan Opera in 1968."

In 1991, Domingo completed his hoped-for 30 years as a professional performer. Rather than resting on his laurels or considering retirement, he was looking for new challenges. Specifically, he was preparing to launch himself into the demanding heldentenor repertory of German opera. He had already sung Wagner's *Lohengrin*, and he had made a recording of the same composer's *Tannhäuser*. Now he was ready to confront one of the most arduous operas ever written, Wagner's *Parsifal*, a complex and somewhat mystical work based on the legend of the knight Parsifal and the quest for the Holy Grail.

"Venturing the title role in *Parsifal*, one of the most musically and dramatically demanding parts Wagner wrote, marks a new level of intensity in Domingo's commitment," wrote Jamie James in *Opera News*. "Making it even more of a gutsy undertaking is the fact that he will sing the role for the first time at the Metropolitan Opera. It is characteristic of Domingo to put all his chips on an all-or-nothing roll." Shortly before the scheduled performance, there were reports in the New York papers that Domingo was having second thoughts and was about to pull out for fear of wrecking his voice. But when the curtain rose at the Met on March 15, Domingo was there onstage.

Once again, Domingo's instincts were correct. "The role of Parsifal proved right for him," wrote critic Donal Henahan in the next day's *New York Times*. "It does not venture very high but it does require just the kind of rich, powerful middle and lower tones that Mr. Domingo commanded all evening. Dramatically, too, one could almost believe in his progress from innocent youth in the first act (no Wagnerian tenor is really credible there, physically or vocally) to weary, middle-aged warrior at the end." Buoyed by the success of this venture, Domingo planned to repeat the role in Vienna. He also decided to add more Wagnerian works to his repertory, including *Tristan und Isolde* and *Die Walküre*. The heldentenor career that eluded his father in the 1930s is within Domingo's reach in the 1990s.

Marta Domingo once said of her husband, "To my Plácido, opera is not a profession. It is in his blood. He loves the music so much, he would need two lives to really enjoy and appreciate it all." After 30 years in opera, Domingo has in a sense had those 2 lives. He has sung well over 2,000 performances and more than 90 different roles—more than twice as much, as he has pointed out on many occasions, as many singers accomplish in an entire career.

And with performances scheduled well into the 1990s, his career is far from over.

Maintaining his ambition to branch out into conducting, Domingo has taken on the post of musical adviser both to the Maestranza in Seville and to the Los Angeles City Center Opera. He hopes that he will eventually conduct opera in both houses and in others as well. He continues to promote zarzuela and other forms of Hispanic music; when he finally gives up singing, he will very likely organize tours and concerts for zarzuela companies and other performers and possibly produce records of Hispanic music.

Finally, he would like to establish a school for aspiring opera singers—a school based on his own beliefs about opera and education. Through rigorous auditions, he would select 20 or 25 young singers from around the world for a 2-year program of preparation

Domingo appears in concert along with conductor Zubin Mehta and violinist Itzhak Perlman. Domingo entered the 1990s with plans for developing his own conducting talents, producing records, and creating an academy for young singers.

and performances. The school would also offer opportunities for young opera conductors and perhaps for set designers and stage directors as well. Domingo would like the school to serve as a forum for educating future audiences as well as future performers. According to his plan, younger children and teenagers would be able to attend performances at the school—but only after learning a little about the operas they were going to hear so that they would have the best possible chance of enjoying the experience.

Domingo's plans for his academy of opera are typically ambitious and exuberant. He would like his school, he says, to "make a big impact on the whole world of opera." Over the course of his singing career, Domingo himself has certainly made such an impact. Through a combination of exceptional talent, faith in himself, and relentless dedication, he has reached the top of a profession as challenging as any in the world.

Selected Recordings and Videos

Since 1969, Plácido Domingo has made nearly 200 recordings of opera and popular music. The partial list that follows includes complete operas (marked with an *), concerts, collections, and popular music.

1969*   *Il trovatore*
         RCA

1970*   *Aïda*
         RCA

1970*   *Don Carlos*
         Angel Records

1971*   *Les Contes d'Hoffmann*
         London Records

1972*   *Norma*
         RCA

1972*   *Manon Lescaut*
         Angel Records

1972   *Domingo Sings Caruso*
         RCA

1972*   *Tosca*
         RCA

1973*   *La Bohème*
         RCA

1974   *Music of My Country* (Zarzuela arias)
            London Records

1975*   *Carmen*
            London Records

1976*   *Die Meistersinger*
            Deutsche Grammophon

1976*   *Andrea Chénier*
            RCA

1976   *Be My Love*
            Deutsche Grammophon

1976*   *La Forza del Destino*
            RCA

1976*   *Macbeth*
            Deutsche Grammophon

1977*   *L'elisir d'amore*
            CBS

1977*   *La fanciulla del West*
            Deutsche Grammophon

1978*   *Faust*
            Angel Records

1978*   *Madama Butterfly*
            CBS

1978*   *Otello*
            RCA

1978   *Romantic Opera Duets*
            CBS

1979*   *Luisa Miller*
            Deutsche Grammophon

1979*   *Rigoletto*
            Deutsche Grammophon

1980   *Plácido Domingo and the Vienna Choirboys*
            RCA

1980*   *Tosca*
            Angel Records

1981*   *Aïda*
         Deutsche Grammophon

1981   *Christmas with Plácido Domingo*
         CBS

1981   *Gala Opera Concert*
         Deutsche Grammophon

1981   *Perhaps Love* (with John Denver)
         CBS

1981   *Tangos*
         Deutsche Grammophon

1981*   *Turandot*
         Deutsche Grammophon

1982*   *La Rondine*
         CBS

1982*   *La Traviata*
         Elektra

1982   *Adoro* (popular Mexican songs)
         CBS

1983*   *Ernani*
         Angel Records

1983   *Always in My Heart*
         CBS

1983   *My Life for a Song*
         CBS

1983*   *Don Carlos*
         Deutsche Grammophon

1986   *Romanzas and Zarzuelas*
         Angel Records

1986*   *Lohengrin*
         London Records

1989   *Domingo at the Philharmonic*
         CBS

1990   *Carreras, Domingo, Pavarotti in Concert*
         London Records

1990*   *Tannhäuser*
        Deutsche Grammophon
1991*   *Aïda*
        RCA
1991   *On Broadway*
        Atlantic

Selected Videos

Domingo has appeared in many television documentaries and opera telecasts that have been released on videotape. The following partial list includes complete operas (marked with an *) as well as recitals, concerts, and documentaries. Many are available for rental from school and public libraries.

1974, 1990* *Madama Butterfly*
1982*   *Cavelleria Rusticana*
1982*   *Ernani*
1982*   *I Pagliacci*
1985*   *Tosca*
1985*   *Il trovatore*
1986*   *La fanciulla del west*
1986   *Live from the Met*
1986*   *Tales of Hoffmann*
1987   *An Evening with Plácido*
1987*   *Andrea Chénier*
1988   *A Year in the Life of Plácido Domingo*
1988*   *Don Carlos*
1988*   *Les Troyens*
1988*   *Manon Lescaut*
1988   *Opera Favorites with Plácido Domingo and Kiri Te Kanawa*
1989*   *L'Africaine*
1989*   *La Gioconda*
1990*   *Aïda*
1990   *Carreras, Domingo, Pavarotti in Concert*
1990   *Great Arias with Plácido Domingo and Friends*
1990   *Songs of Mexico* (2 volumes)
1990*   *Turandot*

Chronology

Jan. 21, 1941	Born Plácido Domingo, Jr., in Madrid, Spain
1946	Parents resettle in Mexico
1948	Domingo travels to Mexico with his sister to join their parents
1949	Begins music studies in Mexico City
1957	Marries first wife
1958	Son José is born
1959	Domingo begins singing with Mexican National Opera; first marriage ends
1961	Domingo makes opera debut as Alfredo in *La traviata* in Monterrey, Mexico; makes U.S. debut in Dallas, Texas
1962	Marries soprano Marta Ornelas; moves to Israel for two and a half years to sing with the Hebrew National Opera
1965	Makes New York City Opera debut; son Plácido is born
1966	Domingo makes Spanish debut in Barcelona
1967	Makes debut at Vienna Staatsoper in *Don Carlos*
1968	Debuts at Metropolitan Opera in New York City in *Adriana Lecouvreur*, son Alvaro is born
1969	Domingo makes debut at La Scala in Milan, Italy, in *Ernani*; records first albums

1971	Makes debut at Covent Garden in London in *Tosca*; passes 700-performance milestone
1973	Makes conducting debut at the New York City Opera
1981	Records *Perhaps Love* album with John Denver
1982	Makes first feature film, *La traviata*
1983	Passes 1,200-performance milestone
1984	Makes conducting debut at the Metropolitan Opera; feature film *Carmen* is released
1985	Earthquake in Mexico City in September kills four Domingo family members; Domingo gives benefit concerts to raise money for earthquake relief
1986	Feature film *Otello* released
1989	Domingo passes the 2,000-performance milestone
1990	Performs with Luciano Pavarotti and José Carreras in Three Tenors concert in Rome
1991	Debuts in *Parsifal* at the Metropolitan Opera
1992	Receives sixth honorary degree from a university (Georgetown)
1993	Founds Operalia, an annual world opera contest
1998	Wins American Latino Media Arts Award (ALMA) for Outstanding Performance in a Music Series
1999	Opens the 1999/2000 season at the Metropolitan Opera, setting the record for season's opening nights with 18
2000	Receives ninth Grammy Award

Further Reading

Allison, Sue. "Plácido." *Life* (October 1989).

Camner, James. *How to Enjoy Opera*. Garden City, NY: Doubleday, 1981.

Davis, Peter G. "Domingo Does Everything." *New York* (September 17, 1984).

———. "It's All There Now for Tenor Plácido Domingo." *New York Times* (March 21, 1977).

———. "Pop Goes Domingo!" *New York* (March 1, 1982).

Domingo, Plácido. *My First Forty Years*. New York: Knopf, 1983.

Duarte, Patricia. "Plácido Domingo." *Nuestro* (August 1980).

Greenfield, Charles. "Spain's King of Tenors." *Nuestro* (March 1985).

Holland, Bernard. "The Well-Tempered Tenor." *New York Times Magazine* (January 30, 1983).

Jacobson, Robert. "What Makes Plácido Run." *Opera News* (March 27, 1982).

James, Jamie. "Pilgrimage." *Opera News* (March 30, 1991).

Orrey, Leslie. *A Concise History of Opera.* New York: Scribners, 1972.

Roos, James. "Work Is Domingo's Peace." *Miami Herald* (January 16, 1983).

Rosenthal, Harold, and John Warrack. *The Concise Oxford Dictionary of Opera.* London: Oxford University Press, 1964.

Rowes, Barbara. "Oh, Luciano! Opera's Other Tenor, Plácido Domingo, Is Hot on Your Heels!" *People* (March 29, 1982).

Scovell, Jane. "Domingo: Giving His Best." *Opera News* (September 1987).

Snowman, Daniel. *The World of Plácido Domingo.* London: Bodley Head, 1985.

Swan, Annalynn. "Bravissimo, Domingo!" *Newsweek* (March 8, 1982).

Walker, Gerald. "The More I Sing, the Better I Sound." *New York Times Magazine* (February 27, 1972).

Webster, Daniel. "New Roles: Plácido Domingo Is Casting His Voice Beyond the Opera House." *Philadelphia Inquirer* (October 29, 1983).

Index

REBECCA STEFOFF is a Philadelphia-based freelance writer and editor who has published more than 40 nonfiction books for young adults. She has also served as the editorial director of Chelsea House's PLACES AND PEOPLES OF THE WORLD and LET'S DISCOVER CANADA series. Stefoff received her M.A. and Ph.D. degrees in English from the University of Pennsylvania, where she taught for three years.

RODOLFO CARDONA is professor of Spanish and comparative literature at Boston University. A renowned scholar, he has written many works of criticism, including *Ramón, a Study of Gómez de la Serna and His Works* and *Visión del esperpento: Teoría y práctica del esperpento en Valle-Inclán.* Born in San José, Costa Rica, he earned his B.A. and M.A. from Louisiana State University and received a Ph.D. from the University of Washington. He has taught at Case Western Reserve University, the University of Pittsburgh, the University of Texas at Austin, the University of New Mexico, and Harvard University.

JAMES COCKCROFT is currently a visiting professor of Latin American and Caribbean studies at the State University of New York at Albany. A three-time Fulbright scholar, he earned a Ph.D. from Stanford University and has taught at the University of Massachusetts, the University of Vermont, and the University of Connecticut. He is the author or coauthor of numerous books on Latin American subjects, including *Neighbors in Turmoil: Latin America, The Hispanic Experience in the United States: Contemporary Issues and Perspectives,* and *Outlaws in the Promised Land: Mexican Immigrant Workers and America's Future.*